Advance Praise for *The No-Cry Discipline Solution*

Finally, a discipline "solution" that offers actual solutions! Elizabeth Pantley doesn't beat around the bush with fancy parenting philosophies and theories. Kids are people, too—and with that simple premise, she lures parents away from heady fantasies of control toward an empathetic understanding of the ups and downs of daily life with young children.

Once parents get a handle on what's going on and why, Pantley offers concrete, easy-to-follow tips for riding out everyday behavioral speed bumps. This feature is what makes Pantley's No-Cry books a godsend for frazzled parents in search of tools they can put to work on the spot. *The No-Cry Discipline Solution* brings problem behavior out of the touchy-feely realm of theory into a more practical realm of "I love you and I want to enjoy my day with you!"—something every parent can relate to.

> —Lisa Poisso, *editor-in-chief, Natural Family Online,*
> *www.naturalfamilyonline.com*

Finally someone wrote a book about discipline in a way that doesn't proselytize or point fingers. It merely points out what we *can* do while loving our children to bits. Reading this book is like receiving a warm embrace from a dear friend. Elizabeth Pantley's tone is nonjudgmental, her approach down-to-earth. You will love it for its nurturing, honest flavor. *The No-Cry Discipline Solution* is a gift to every parent who suffers from guilt and shame for being (gasp!) human.

> —Christine Louise Hohlbaum, *parenting humorist and*
> *author of* Diary of a Mother *and* SAHM I Am:
> Tales of a Stay-at-Home Mom in Europe

Elizabeth Pantley is an expert on gentle, mindful parenting, and *The No-Cry Discipline Solution* exemplifies her knowledge and ability to manifest her expertise in a practical, readable text. Pantley not only helps us to become more conscious of our children's needs and perspectives but allows us to embrace their uniqueness and find a discipline technique that works for each child. But, more importantly, Pantley helps us to become more aware of ourselves as parents—our weaknesses, doubts, and fears—and thereby empowers us to grow and develop our parenting skills, moving beyond discipline into the creation of family harmony. *The No-Cry Discipline Solution* should be required reading for parents everywhere!

—*Nancy Massotto, Ph.D., executive director,*
Holistic Moms Network

Many books about child discipline focus on making children conform. Elizabeth Pantley allows us to see child behavior through their young eyes. At the same time, she offers solid and usable tips and solutions for parents to help them deal with a range of discipline issues. *The No-Cry Discipline Solution* is parent-friendly and child-friendly. It will be a well-thumbed addition to any parent library.

—*Kathy Lynn, president, Parenting Today,*
www.parentingtoday.ca; parenting speaker; and author of
Who's in Charge Anyway? *and* But Nobody Told Me
I'd Ever Have to Leave Home

Discipline is one of the most discussed areas of parenting, and we all want to get it "right" but too often feel guilty when it all goes wrong. In *The No-Cry Discipline Solution*, Elizabeth Pantley goes about removing this guilt and gives parents great tips on disciplining with less heartache and stress for the parent and child.

Pantley's books are known for their gentle and child-centered approach, and this one is no different. She shows that understanding children for what they are and having realistic expectations of them is vital before we even begin thinking about discipline.

I am not sure that I have read another parenting book on discipline where anger in the parent is discussed so openly and honestly. It is something that we would all pretend does not happen, but Pantley brings it out in the open and helps parents deal with this little-talked-about topic.

This book is an invaluable tool—easy to read and filled with wonderful, practical examples of dealing with common everyday problems. A must-read for all parents!

—Sally Cameron-Zurich, co-owner, www.earthbabies.co.za, a South African parenting website promoting natural baby care and parenting

In *The No-Cry Discipline Solution*, Elizabeth Pantley helps us examine our old discipline ways and teaches us mutually respectful new ideas in her trademark warm, motivating, and humorous way. Once again, Pantley delivers!

—Judy Arnall, *author of* Discipline Without Distress: 135 Tools for Raising Caring, Responsible Children Without Time-Out, Spanking, Punishment, or Bribery, www.professionalparenting.ca

When I read Elizabeth Pantley's new book, I was struck by how parents all over the world struggle with the same everyday battles. As an editor and journalist at *We Parents*, the biggest parent magazine in Sweden, I encounter questions every day regarding these issues.

I consider *The No-Cry Discipline Solution* a toolbox filled with creative solutions for those everyday battles. Of course, there is no single solution that suits everyone, but this book contains so many different solutions to choose from that you're sure to find a solution to suit your own family.

Pantley writes about situations that all parents will recognize. And she writes so that parents will understand the child's point of view. Included in her "toolbox" are explanations as to why a child may behave as he or she does, because in order to solve a problem the best way, a parent should know the underlying causes.

I can truly recommend this book to all parents and parents-to-be. It should have a place of honor on every parent's bookshelf. By reading this book your everyday life with your child will surely become easier, more fun, and more loving.

—*Anna-Maria Stawreberg, editor and reporter,* Vi Föräldrar (We Parents)

If you have ever wondered how to sort out the small stuff from the big stuff of raising children, Elizabeth Pantley helps you do just that. She offers strategies to let go of frustration and guilt over little mishaps, while providing wise counsel and clear direction to raise responsible and loved children. Suggestions are offered to help explore parental attitudes, to better encourage positive child behavior, and to deal with specific challenges. *The No-Cry Discipline Solution* is your family bible for child guidance.

—*Patricia Morgan, counselor and author of* Love Her As She Is: Lessons from a Daughter Stolen by Addictions

An A-to-Z manual for all parents encountering the abundant challenges and complications in raising children. Elizabeth Pantley's honest and realistic approach in *The No-Cry Discipline Solution* in dealing with troublesome behavior offers parents fun-loving and gentle ways of dealing with discipline.

—*Azmina Hansraj, editor, www.baby-mates.com,* London, United Kingdom

the no-cry
discipline solution

Also by Elizabeth Pantley:

The No-Cry Potty Training Solution (2006)
The No-Cry Sleep Solution for Toddlers and Preschoolers (2005)
Gentle Baby Care (2004)
The No-Cry Sleep Solution (2002)
Hidden Messages (2001)
Perfect Parenting (1999)
Kid Cooperation (1996)

Contributor, with Dr. William and Martha Sears:

The Successful Child (2002)

the no-cry discipline solution

Gentle Ways to Encourage Good Behavior
Without Whining, Tantrums & Tears

Elizabeth Pantley

Bestselling author of *The No-Cry Sleep Solution*

New York   Chicago   San Francisco   Lisbon   London   Madrid   Mexico City
Milan   New Delhi   San Juan   Seoul   Singapore   Sydney   Toronto

Library of Congress Cataloging-in-Publication Data

Pantley, Elizabeth.
    The no-cry discipline solution : gentle ways to encourage good behavior without whining, tantrums, and tears / by Elizabeth Pantley.
       p.   cm.
    ISBN 0-07-147159-6
    1. Discipline of children.   2. Parenting.   I. Title.

HQ770.4.P364   2007
649'.64—dc22   2006036815

1 2 3 4 5 6 7 8 9 10 11 12 13 14 15 16 17 18 19 20 21 DOC/DOC 0 9 8 7

ISBN-13: 978-0-07-147159-6
ISBN-10:   0-07-147159-6

McGraw-Hill books are available at special quantity discounts to use as premiums and sales promotions, or for use in corporate training programs. For more information, please write to the Director of Special Sales, Professional Publishing, McGraw-Hill, Two Penn Plaza, New York, NY 10121-2298. Or contact your local bookstore.

This book is designed to provide parents and caregivers with a variety of ideas and suggestions. It is sold with the understanding that the publisher and the author are not rendering psychological, medical, or professional services. It is also sold with the understanding that the author is not a doctor or psychologist and that the information in this book is the author's opinion, unless otherwise stated. Questions and comments attributed to parents represent a compilation and adaptation of letters from many readers, unless indicated otherwise. This material is presented without any warranty or guarantee of any kind, express or implied, including but not limited to the implied warranties of merchantability or fitness for a particular purpose. It is not possible to cover every eventuality in any answer, and the reader should always consult a professional for individual needs. Readers should bring their child to a doctor or medical care provider for regular checkups and bring any questions they have to a medical professional. In regard to every topic included herein, this book is not a substitute for competent professional health care or professional counseling.

This book is printed on acid-free paper.

This book is dedicated with love to my sisters,
Renée and Michelle
With fond memories from long ago
And joyful times still today
A lifetime of friendship
All those days we spent talking, sharing, hugging
And laughing, laughing, always laughing
Watching them
As women, strong and capable
And as mothers, so warm, so loving, so nurturing
With the comfort of knowing
That no matter what
That we will always be the very best of friends

I love you, my sisters.

Contents

Foreword

Discipline can be an overwhelming and complicated subject for parents. The idea that we are responsible for helping our children successfully make the journey from infancy to adulthood can be a frightening concept. But the word *discipline* simply means to teach, and, as parents, we teach our children every day through our words, actions, and example.

In *The No-Cry Discipline Solution*, Elizabeth Pantley shows how we can effectively help our children master the practical skills necessary for learning. She demonstrates that a parent's actions are only part of the discipline equation; the second half is the child's act of learning. She provides many concrete methods for helping young children learn and grow into self-disciplined individuals. She also provides parents with reassurance and achievable methods for managing discipline in everyday life with children.

Pantley says that "Parental discipline is about helping our children create a foundation of strong values, morals, and guidelines that they can use for a lifetime of self-discipline." It is the job of parents, teachers, and other influential adults to provide children with the tools and guidance they need to develop this self-discipline. A job of this magnitude is best not left to chance or inexperience. Any adult who is responsible in any part for raising a child would be wise to read, study, and learn how best to approach this exceptionally important undertaking.

True to the heart of all of Pantley's No-Cry books, this volume shows parents how to help children be receptive to the lessons they teach by avoiding the tears, frustration, and anger that serve as barriers to learning. It explains the underlying emotions and motivations that drive a child's behavior and shows how to use this knowledge to guide a child to make the right choices.

As a parent educator and mother of four children, Pantley has the wisdom and experience to blend professional knowledge with realistic, practical advice. Her methods are clearly explained, and they are demonstrated with many understandable examples. The helpful tips and stories from her vast group of test parents add even more practicality to the tools provided.

The No-Cry Discipline Solution is a definite must-have for all parents and caregivers of young children. If you are looking for understandable, effective, and nurturing tools to raise good human beings, let this book be your guide.

—Tim Seldin

About Tim Seldin

Tim Seldin is president of the Montessori Foundation and chair of the International Montessori Council. He is the author of several books on Montessori Education. His newest book is *How to Raise an Amazing Child the Montessori Way.* Seldin is the father of five and the grandfather of one. He lives in Florida with his wife, Joyce St. Giermaine.

Acknowledgments

I would like to express my heartfelt appreciation to the many people who lift me up every day with their compassionate support:

Judith McCarthy, my editor, and every person who helps to create my books at McGraw-Hill Publishing: absolutely the best publisher ever.

Meredith Bernstein of The Meredith Bernstein Literary Agency: counselor, friend, and agent extraordinaire.

Patti Hughes: my incredible, enthusiastic, and loveable assistant.

My husband, Robert: my partner, friend, and soul mate.

My family, my joy: Mom, Angela, Vanessa, David, Coleton, Michelle, Loren, Sarah, Nicholas, Renée, Tom, Matthew, Devin, Tyler, and Amber.

All the readers who have written to me about their precious children; I feel a special friendship with every one.

My many test mommies, test daddies, and test children for sharing a piece of their lives with me.

The Test Parents

During the creation of this book, I worked with an incredible group of test parents. The test mommies and daddies, as I affectionately call them, became my friends during this long and complicated process, and I believe I learned as much from them as they learned from me. These 242 people were kind enough, and motivated enough, to complete extensive surveys, answer questions, and participate in polls. They read through the manuscript, applied what they learned, and then reported back to me on a regular basis. They asked questions, and they provided helpful ideas. They let me peek into their families' discipline problems and happy successes.

The test parents live all over the world, and they represent all different kinds of families: married, single, unmarried partners, from one child up to six children, twins, adopted children, young parents, older parents, at-home moms, at-home dads, working parents, interracial families, multicultural families, gay families, and several grandparents-as-parents. They are a varied and interesting group.

Locations
- **160 from the United States:** Alabama, Arizona, California, Colorado, Connecticut, District of Columbia, Florida, Georgia, Illinois, Indiana, Louisiana, Maryland, Massachusetts, Michigan, Missouri, Nevada, New Hampshire, New Jersey, New Mexico, New York, Ohio, Pennsylvania, Rhode Island, South Carolina, South Dakota, Texas, Utah, Vermont, Virginia, Washington
- **28 from Canada:** Alberta, British Columbia, Chilliwack, Manitoba, Nova Scotia, Ontario, Quebec, Saskatchewan, Yellowknife
- **17 from the United Kingdom:** Abingdon, Aldershot, Andover, Bristol, Devon, East Sussex, Hampshire, Newark, Surrey, Leicestershire, Nottinghamshire, Wales
- **9 from Israel:** Hadera, Jerusalem, Modiin, Moshav Olesh, Nof Ayalon, Ramat Gan, Tel Aviv
- **5 from New Zealand:** Cambridge, Hibiscus Coast, Huntsbury, Lower Hutt, Whangarei
- **5 from Australia:** Canberra, Deception Bay, Melbourne, Victoria, Umina
- **3 from Saudi Arabia:** Dammam Eastern, Hail
- **3 from Bahrain:** Diraz, Manama
- **2 from France:** Nates, Haute Savoie
- **2 from Mexico:** D.F., Guatemala City

- **2 from Brazil:** Belo Horizonte, Minas Gerais
- **2 from South Africa:** Atlasville, Cape Town
- **1 from Iceland:** Keflavik
- **1 from Ireland:** Athenry
- **1 from Japan:** Tachikawa
- **1 from Russia:** Moscow

Children

- 202 Girls
- 209 Boys
- 4 sets of Twins
- 247 Toddlers (12 months to 3 years)
- 142 Preschoolers (3 years to 6 years)
- 22 School-Aged Children (7 years to 10 years)

I would like to express my gratitude and affection to every one of my test mommies, test daddies, and their children: Aanyah, Aaron, Abby, Abigail, Adam, Adren, Aeryn, AhLana, Aidan, Aisling, AJ, Aja, Alan, Aleksandar, Alexander, Aliza, Allen, Ally, Amanda, Amani Elizabeth, Amara, Amber, Ameila, Amelia Jun-Die, Amy, Andra, Andreia, Andrew, Aneese, Angela, Angelique, Ann, Anna, Anne-Marie, Annette, Annie, Annik, Arabella Mia, Ariana, Arianna, Ariella, Arley, Asher, Ashlea, Asphyxia, Auila-lei, Aurora, Ava, Avery, Avital, Axa Elisabeth, Aylitamae, Aysha, Bader, Bailey, Barb, Barbara, Basil, Beatrix, Beckie, Becky, Ben, Benjamin, Bennett, Benny, Bethany, Betsy, Bill, Bittani, Blaze, Bobbie, Bonnie, Brandy, Brian, Brianna, Bridget, Brinley, Britt, Brittany Alexis, Brooke, Bruce, Caden, Callum, Candace, Car-ley, Carole, Caroline, Carter, Caspar, Catherine, Chana, Chester, Choshen, Christian, Christine, Christion, Christy, Ciara, Cindy, Claire, Clayton, Clement, Cole, Conall, Connor, Constanze, Corrine, Cristina, Dakari, Dakota, Dale, Damien, Damon, Dan-iel, Danielle, David, Deandra, Deanna, Debbie, Deborah, Deion, Devan, Devanie, Diana, Diana, Diogo Souki, Dionna, Dominique,

Donna, Donovan, Doreen, Dovi, Dylan, Eithan, Ekatarina, Elana, Eleanor, Eleese, Elena, Eli, Elias, Elijah, Eliot, Elise, Elizabeth, Ella, Elliot, Emaya, Emerson, Emily, Emma, Emmett, Erin, Esther, Ethan, Eva, Evalin Julie, Evan, Ezia, Faith, Felicia, Flynn, Frances, Gabi, Gabriel, Gabriela, Gabrielle, Gale, Garrett, Gary, Genevieve, George, Gino, Gracie, Graciela, Graeme, Grayson, Greg, Hadar, Hadley, Hailey, Halene Isabelle, Hannah, Heidi, Henry III, Holly, Ian, Iftach, Isabel, Isabella, Isadora, Isla, Jack, Jackson, Jacob, Jacqueline, Jacquelyn, Jaimie, Jameel, Jamie, Jane, Janell, Janice, Janie, Janos, Jason, Jayda, Jaylah, Jazmine, Jen, Jenna, Jennifer, Jesse, Jessica, Jessie, Jim, Joanne, Jobe, Jocelyn, Jodie, Joe, Joel, John, Jolene, Jordan, Jose, Josef, Joseph, Josh, Joshua, Jubal, Judy, Juliana, Juliane, Julie, Julietta, Kaitlyn, Kalani, Kara, Karah, Karen, Kari, Karolyn, Katherine, Kathi, Kathryn, Katie, Kayla, Kaylie, Keara, Keelin, Kekoa, Kelly, Ken, Kendra, Khalid, Khidar, Kia, Kieron, Kim, Kimberly, Kinder, Kirsten, Krista, Kristi, Kyleigh, Kylie, Laetitia, Langston, Laura, Lauren, Leanne, Lee, Leigh, Liam, Liat, Lila, Lili, Lily, Linda, Lindsay, Lindsey, Liora, Lisa, Liz, Loddie, Logan, Lois, Lorenzo, Lorna, Lorraine, Louise, Lucas, Lucie, Lucy, Luis, Luke, Lynee, Maayan, Mackenzie, Maddison, Maddy, Madeline, Madelyn, Madison, Maia, Maisha, Malachy, Malcolm, Mara, Marc Jonah, Marcie, Margaret, Margot, Mari, Marianna, Marianne, Maribel, Marie, Marin, Marisa, Marissa, Mark, Marlee, Marlo, Mary, Mason, Mathieau, Mati, Matthew, Maverick, Max, Maya, Megan, Meilin, Mel, Meleila, Melissa, Melvin, Menachem, Michael, Michel, Michelle, Miguel, Mike, Mila, Miles, Mira, Miriam, Misha, Molly, Monica, Mordechai, Morgan, Moshe, Myles, Natalia, Natalie, Natasha, Nathan, Neko, Nicholas, Nicole, Nikki, Noa, Noah, Noreen, Ole, Olga, Oliver, Olivia, Omar, Orrin, Osama, Oscar, Paige, Pamela, Patti, Phylicia, Pnina, Prophet, Rachael, Rachelle, Raizel, Ransom, Raymond, Reagan, Rebecca, Renee, Rhonda, Ric, Rina, Rivka, Rohana, Romi, Rory, Rosa, Rosalee, Rosie, Rosina, Ross, Rus, Ryan, Sachin, Safiya, Sage,

Saige, Sakina, Sam, Samantha Belle, Samuel, Sara, Sarah, Sean, Sedona, Sekou, Seth, Shaila, Shamshon, Sharalyn, Sharon, Sheila, Shelley, Sheri, Sherisse, Sherry, Shmuel, Shooni, Simeon, Simon, Singer, Skye, Skyler, Sofia, Solanne Bianchi, Sonja, Sophie, Spencer, Stacey, Stanley, Stephanie, Strahnn, Suzanne, Tara, Tasneem, Taylor, Theo, Theresa, Thomas, Tiane, Tiffany, Timmy, Timothy, Tina, Tobias, Tomas, Toni, Tonia, Tracy, Treston Hart, Tristan, Troy, Umar, Umar, Valeria, Victoria, Vincenzo, Wanda, Waylon, Wendy, Wiley Dennison, Will, William, Willow, Xenia, Yaffa, Yasmin Walters, Yedidya, Yenny, Yolanda, Yonathan, Yoni, Yonina, Yusuf, Zack, Zahava, Zane, Zayd, Zion, Zoe.

Part 1

The Foundation for
No-Cry Discipline: Essential
Parenting Attitudes

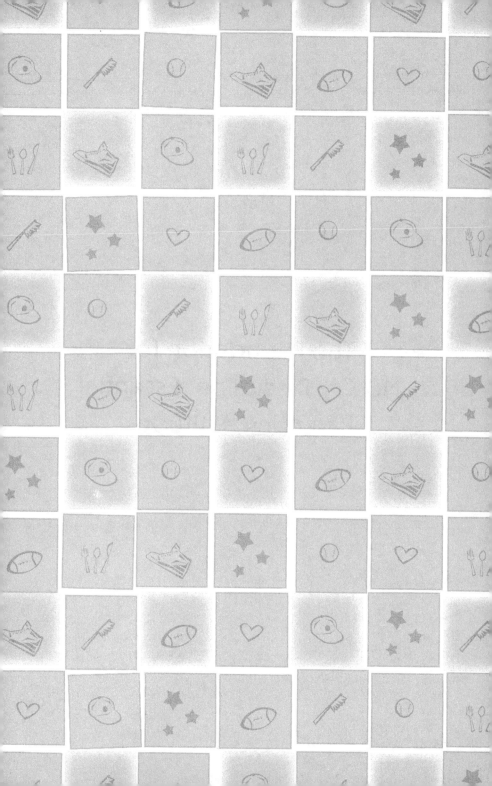

Discipline

A Complex Job Made Easier with the Right Outlook

Raising your children may be the most wonderful and rewarding job of your life. However, when it comes to discipline, it can also be the most complicated, challenging, and frustrating profession in the world. Just the word *discipline* is enough to make many parents cringe as it stirs up visions of a strict parent doling out punishment and a crying child sitting in the corner. But discipline is not about punishment, and it doesn't have to result in tears. As defined by Webster's, *discipline* means "training that develops self-control and character." This definition might lead you to believe that the process is all about teaching, and in a sense it is. Teaching is your part of the discipline equation, and there is no substitute for quality lessons. However, your child's part of the equation is the most important—learning.

My oldest child, Angela, is now eighteen years old and in college. Her dad and I vividly recall an inspirational moment that occurred when she was seven years old. She was trying to explain something important to him and questioned his attention. He said, "I'm listening." To which Angela replied, "Dad, you listen, but you don't understand." It was an enlightening moment for Mom and Dad, and that simple exchange has popped up in many conversations through the years as we raise our four children. We want to understand them, and we want them to understand us as we go about the many lessons we must teach them. Teaching that falls on deaf ears is lost, and we have learned that crying plugs a child's

Key Point

"Education is the kindling of a flame, not the filling of a vessel."

—Socrates, Ancient Greek philosopher

ears almost every time it occurs. Crying gets in the way of accepting, understanding, and learning.

Parental discipline is about helping our children create a foundation of strong values, morals, and guidelines that they can use for a lifetime of self-discipline. The teaching of these principles occurs with nearly every exchange we have with our children. *No-cry discipline* means helping children be receptive to the lessons you teach by avoiding the tears and anger that serve as a barrier to learning.

None of us are born knowing how to be a parent, nor how to go about teaching our children important life lessons. Most of us find that this job is much more complex than we ever dreamed it would be. Taking care of a baby is our first step on the journey of parenthood, and the lessons that we teach during the baby years are about love, connection, and basic human interaction. Just when we feel confident with our skills and ideals for raising babies, we turn around to find that many of those skills that we've learned do not apply to a walking, talking toddler. We adjust our approach, only to find that disrupted when our toddler turns into a preschooler, and again when he becomes a grade-schooler, and again when he enters the teen years . . . and yet again when our child graduates and moves on to college or adult life. There is no *stop* button for when your parenting job ends; once a child enters your life you remain a parent forever. We actually have a *brand-new* parenting job each time our child passes from one milestone

Derryn, age 2, and Wade, age 4

to another in his life. Just like any other undertaking, the more knowledge you have at each step of the way, the more confident you will feel, the easier your job will be, and the better your lifelong relationship will be with your child.

There are many things you can do to enhance your enjoyment of being a parent. There are many things you can do to avoid the blockades of anger and tears, things that allow discipline to unfold in its most effective way. Practiced skills and set guidelines can help you move from milestone to milestone with relative ease. These ideas can help you raise your child to be open to learning and to become a wonderful human being. You can discover these parenting skills on your own; they can be learned on the job through trial and error. However, the "error" part can be prolonged and painful. Or, you can learn effective skills by analyzing and studying the successes (and failures) of the masses of other parents who have gone before you.

It can help to begin your journey by examining your own feelings about discipline and your feelings about what it means to be a parent. You can set off on the right road when you expel the negative beliefs that dampen your spirits and then fill that space with positive, effective parenting skills.

Banish the Myths

As if it isn't challenging enough to raise children, most parents believe myths that complicate the process by making them feel confused, frustrated, and inadequate. These horrible myths become dark, nearly suffocating clouds that hover over them, spoiling the joy of the child-rearing experience.

There is an oft-repeated quote by John Wilmot, Earl of Rochester, who said, "Before I got married, I had six theories about bringing up children. Now I have six children and no theories." All of us have theories, ideals, and expectations about parenting before we raise our own children. But once we become parents, we learn through experience that many of these turn out to be completely wrong. Sometimes these beliefs are naïve or misguided; sometimes they're total fabrications.

Here is a quiz to help you determine which common and distressing myths you believe. You may have never realized how intensely these beliefs affect you, but they do. After you identify the myths that color your daily life, I'll share the truth about each one. By acknowledging that these myths exist in your life, you take the first step toward eliminating them. Learning the truth will erase your doubts and leave you open to learning effective new ways of raising your children.

Indicate with an honest Yes or No if you believe (or have ever believed) the following statements:

YES	NO	Parenting Belief
____	____	If a parent is truly attached, committed, and connected to a child, then that child will naturally behave properly; discipline won't be necessary.

____	____	If you love your child and if your intentions are good, parenting will come naturally to you.
____	____	Good parents don't lose their patience and shout at their children.
____	____	If parents are a perfectly matched couple and have a strong relationship, they will agree about how to raise their children.
____	____	Parents are totally responsible for their child's behavior and actions. Outstanding parenting means that children will turn out well.
____	____	If you read parenting books, take classes, and learn effective skills and tools, you will always be in control. Once you learn all the correct parenting approaches, your life as a parent will be trouble-free.

Now that you've taken a minute to assess your parenting beliefs, let's take the time to dispel those myths so that you can reduce any anxiety and guilt you may be having over imaginary problems. In addition, you may be able to prevent future problems when you sift through the falsehoods and truths of parenthood. According to Candace B. Pert, Ph.D., in her book *Everything You Need to Know to Feel Go(o)d* (Hay House, 2006), "We all use imagery every day when we engage in the two most common forms of worry: either regretting the past or fearing the future . . . [but] we can use that same ability in a more positive way." She goes on to say, "The more you bring your attention, or conscious awareness, to something you intend to manifest, the more likely that intention will become real in the world." So, let's now look at each myth and the genuine truth and move forward to more uncluttered, positive parenting.

Myth: If a parent is truly attached, committed, and connected to a child, then that child will naturally behave properly; discipline won't be necessary.

Father-Speak

"We always thought that good parenting would mean that our child would not fuss and have tantrums. Boy, were we wrong. It was almost harder to deal with the fact that despite our devoted parenting style our child was having tantrums than it was to deal with the actual tantrums."

—Adam, father to Zahava, age 4

Truth: You could be totally committed to your child from the moment of birth. You could read all the best parenting books. You could take parenting classes. You could do absolutely *everything* right. In fact, you could be a truly magnificent, spectacular, utterly faultless saint, and your child would *still* misbehave. The truth is *all* children misbehave. *All* children make mistakes. *All* children will whine, fuss, and have temper tantrums. This is true because all children are human beings—*young, inexperienced, naïve human beings.* And to be human is to be fallible—to make mistakes, to make poor decisions, and, hopefully, to learn from these.

When a child fails to behave, it is not a reflection of a parent's lack of commitment or skill. It is not an indication that the child is lacking in any way. It is simply a facet of our humanness.

It is our duty and privilege to love our children and to guide and direct them, to be committed to them, and to be devoted to parenting them in the best way we can. And it is our duty to understand that our children *are* perfect—a realistic, human perfection that allows for mistakes and misbehavior along the way to growth and development. These mistakes are necessary to ensure that learning and growth take place, and that is the beauty of parenting. Our children do not have to be flawless to receive our unconditional love and support.

Myth: If you love your child and if your intentions are good, parenting will come naturally to you.

Truth: Loving your child is easy. Raising your child is hard. Effective parenting skills are *learned*. Raising children is complicated, intense, and ever changing. In order to be a calm, effective parent you need knowledge and skills, and it's a very rare person who innately possesses these skills.

This concept is made even more complicated because there are no distinct black-and-white answers when it comes to raising children, and contradictory advice abounds. So parents must sort through everything they know, everything they hear, and everything they learn to come up with the right parenting approach for each of their children.

Mother-Speak

"This is one of those myths that I believed totally, so I lost complete faith in myself when faced with my first son's misbehavior. I looked for answers from everyone and anyone, and then I was left confused when I obtained totally conflicting advice. It has taken me two more children to finally figure out that all children have their unpleasant moments. Now, I believe in myself, read about things I have doubts on, and follow only the advice that makes sense to me."

—Janie, mother to Grayson, age 4; Emerson, age 3; and Anna, age 2

Myth: Good parents don't lose their patience and shout at their children.

Truth: Even the most peaceful, easygoing parent loses patience and yells from time to time—we are all human. No matter how much we love our children, they will try our patience, they will make mistakes, and they will bring us to anger.

All children have their "naughty" moments. And, guess what? When children are "naughty," parents lose their patience and—gasp!—they YELL.

I am an experienced mom of four. I make my living writing books and giving lectures about how to raise children. I love my children with my whole heart and soul, and I try my best to be a good mother. Yet . . . my children misbehave. My six-year-old son misbehaves, and my three teenagers *still* misbehave. And, more often than I'd like, when my children misbehave . . . I lose my patience and I yell. Just like you. Just like every single parent in the entire world.

So what do you say we kill this oppressive myth? We should stand up and shout, "Human beings make mistakes! Parents and children are human beings! Kids sometimes misbehave! Parents sometimes yell! That is NORMAL!"

Myth: If parents are a perfectly matched couple and have a strong relationship, they will agree about how to raise their children.

Truth: It's very common for two parents, even those who are perfectly matched and in a happy relationship, to disagree about child-rearing approaches. Some may disagree about baby care issues, yet others will be perfectly in sync during the baby years and then find they are at odds when their child becomes old enough for school or enters the teen years.

The way that we approach child-rearing is influenced by our past experiences—both the things we choose to do and the things we try to avoid. It is nearly impossible for two people to be in perfect agreement on every parenting decision. But, good communication and ongoing discussion can help any couple find agreement on important issues as they raise their children.

Mother-Speak

"I have noticed many times that when my husband starts to discipline our son, I jump in and try to make what he has done seem not as bad. For some reason I get this maternal urge to save him. Save him from what? I think about it later and realize that he was misbehaving and his daddy was correcting him, so no saving was necessary! Even though we are using the same technique, we use different verbal and nonverbal approaches. That maternal instinct is always right there, but I have to continue to make an effort to let it go because my way is not the only way. I can see that Garrett is responding very well to the consistency of both of us in our separate ways."

—**Brandy, mother to Garrett, age 2**

Even when we agree on basic fundamental parenting theory, we might slightly disagree on approach. And, even if we agree on approach, our differing personalities guarantee that we won't always handle things in exactly the same way.

Myth: Parents are totally responsible for their child's behavior and actions. Outstanding parenting means that children will turn out well.

Truth: Just as adults' personalities are different, so are children's. Even when two children are raised in exactly the same way, in the same house, and with the same parents, their unique personalities plus their different perceptions of life affect how they interpret their worlds. They can become very different people. It is true that a parent's actions can greatly influence behavior—but personality

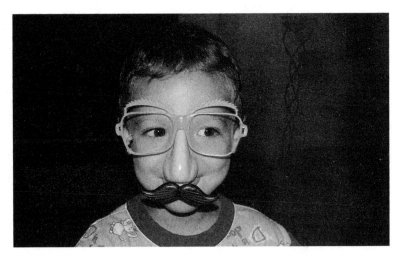

Wade, age 4

plus life experiences outside the family have an impact on how a child responds in any given situation.

Parents are not 100 percent responsible for every action their child takes. Children are separate human beings from their parents, and from a young age their decisions begin to affect the path they will take in life. Children are not a blank slate upon which we

Father-Speak

"My brothers and I were all raised the same way, but we are three distinctly different people, with very dissimilar personalities and traits. We are so different that some people are surprised to find out that we're even brothers."

—David, father to Brian, age 6, and Josh, age 3

can write whatever we choose, nor are they a piece of clay we can mold into any shape we desire. However, parents do matter, and they matter a great deal. How you raise your children will make an influential impact on the adult that your child becomes. There is a definite relationship between the way you raise your children and the level of happiness and success they will achieve in life. Positive, thoughtful, effective parenting has the greatest chance of reaping the reward of successful, happy children with healthy self-esteem who grow into successful, happy adults who experience a satisfying life.

Myth: If you read parenting books, take classes, and learn effective skills and tools, you will always be in control. Once you learn all the correct parenting approaches, your life as a parent will be trouble-free.

Truth: Parents are people, and people are not perfect. No matter how many wonderful skills we have, no matter how much knowledge we have, there will be many times when our emotions interfere and we don't react in the best ways. As a matter of fact, the more we know, the more critical we are of ourselves. We begin to see the mistakes more clearly and judge our own faults more harshly. The best parents are the ones who try the hardest, yet they judge themselves by the strictest guidelines.

Key Point

Everyone needs help as they raise children. No one should parent in a vacuum—we should take advantage of the many wonderful resources available to guide us, but with the understanding that we cannot possibly apply everything we learn every day. We can just do our best.

Key Point

Parents who do the right thing 70 percent of the time should feel proud of the job they are doing.

Keep in mind that children are people, too. They have volatile emotions, varying moods, and plenty of needs and wants. And children change and grow from day to day as they learn about themselves and their world.

To aim for 100 percent perfection in parenting is an impossible goal. Seventy percent is about as perfect as you can get as a parent. This percentage can result in a happy family. Even with the usual bumps and bad moments, 70 percent will result in children who turn out well.

Key Point

"Do not believe in what you have heard; do not believe in traditions because they have been handed down for many generations; do not believe anything because it is rumored and spoken of by many; do not believe merely because the written statements of some old sage are produced; do not believe in conjectures; do not believe in that as a truth to which you have become attached by habit; do not believe merely on the authority of your teachers and elders.

"After observation and analysis, when it agrees with reason and is conducive to the good and benefit of one and all, then accept it and live up to it."

—Buddha (2,600 years ago)

Take some time to think about these and other myths, theories, ideals, and expectations that you have believed. Ponder where these beliefs originated and why you believe them to be true. Then contemplate what you are learning about the truth of the matter. When you analyze myths and replace them with your own truth, it can help you to approach parenting in a more honest, uncluttered, and enjoyable way.

Planning Ahead,
Looking Ahead
Your Child as a Teenager

I recently lectured at a conference for childbirth educators. The theme was "Preparing Expectant Parents for the Realities of Life with Baby." The organizers told me that the theme was chosen because one of the most common challenges educators report is that parents put a great deal more time and energy into decorating the nursery and buying baby clothes than into thinking about what life with their baby will really be like. Consequently, the most common complaints that new parents have are: "I didn't know what to expect!" "No one ever told me raising a baby would be so hard!" "I feel clumsy, confused, and inadequate." The reality of life with a new baby shines a beacon on the fact that the color of the nursery walls and the number of cute outfits in the dresser have nothing whatsoever to do with how confident, capable, or prepared a first-time parent is in his or her new role.

It is the same manner of thinking that causes many parents of young children to believe that it's much too early to be thinking ahead to when their children are teens—or even sixth graders. Here is a time when my personal experience as a mother allows me an inspired understanding. My youngest child is a kindergartener. My older three children are teenagers—my oldest just beginning college. This blend of ages is a blessing in my work as a parenting educator—I can see both ends of the parenting spectrum.

Just as childbirth educators believe that understanding baby care *before* the baby comes home gives parents the knowledge for coping with the challenges they meet *after* the baby comes, I believe that looking ahead to the time when your child will be a young adult will provide you with tremendous guidance and insight as you raise your young child today. Give yourself an opportunity to look to the future for a bit of emotional time travel, and, *before* that future arrives, ask yourself, *What would I have done differently?*

As a mother of an eighteen-year-old just off to college and two other teenagers who are soon on their way plus a six-year-old son with whom I'm immersed in daily life, I have asked myself these questions: *What would I have done differently with my older three children? What will I do differently with my youngest? How might I approach parenting if another baby were to enter my life?* Putting aside any trivial issues (for instance, I would have created a shoe cubby much sooner), this book allows me to share my most important realizations and lessons with you.

Looking Ahead, Then Looking Back: What Would *You* Have Done Differently That You Can Change Now?

Luckily, I am able to see with open eyes, make corrections, and use what I have learned as I continue to raise my children. And, even more, I'm able to share these thoughts with you. Of course, not every parent has the same goals, values, or personality that I do. And each of you will create your own list, in time. However, what's most important right now is to simply take the time to envision your child as a young adult. Capture the most important traits and values you hope to see in that beautiful person as well as the relationship you will have with that incredible human being.

Use your vision to guide you as you make the most important decisions in your daily life. This is an ongoing process that requires updating from time to time, but by keeping one eye on the future you will make better decisions today.

How Today's Actions Will Affect Your Future Teenager

We cannot totally mold our child into the person we want him or her to be, of course. However, the ways that we respond to our babies, toddlers, and preschoolers will directly affect the way they will be as school-age children, which, in turn, will affect who they become as teenagers and later as adults. When it comes to the typical misconduct that parents of teenagers struggle with, the seeds of those behaviors were planted way, way, *way* back—when the teen was a baby and toddler. Those seeds were unintentionally watered and fertilized during the preschool and early childhood years until they became sturdy plants (or actually more like overgrown weeds that become very difficult to deal with).

If you could get a glimpse of your children as they will be in the future, it would provide enlightenment and give you tremendous guidance as you move through your days. You can't do that, but you don't really have to. Since all children are remarkably similar in many behaviors, you can gain the benefit of those families who have gone before you to plant the seeds for a more positive and pleasant future. Listed in the chart that follows are some specific examples of unpleasant teen behavior, compared to the preferred behavior, along with tips on how you can increase the odds your child will grow into a teenager and young adult who demonstrates the good behavior all parents hope for.

This chart shows only a few of the most common and frustrating behaviors; of course, it's not a complete picture of everyday life. The list could go on for many more pages, filling an entire book! However, if you can begin to open your mind beyond the moment and look to where you and your child are headed in the future, you'll be able to make better, more effective parenting decisions. Every single time? Every single day? No, not by a long shot! Life is complicated and days with children are hectic, but when you have guiding lights along your path, the end result is always, always better.

Typical Older Child/Teenager Misbehavior	Preferred Behavior	How to Help Your Young Child Develop the Preferred Behavior
Leaves dirty dishes all over the house	Puts dishes in dishwasher, runs it, and then puts the dishes away	**Toddler:** Have him hand his dish to you when done eating. **Preschooler:** Have him put his own dishes on the counter or in the sink. **Child:** Have him put dishes in the dishwasher, help unload and put dishes away, and follow a cleanup routine.
Leaves piles of dirty clothes on bedroom floor	Launders clothes and puts them away	**Toddler:** Have her carry her own clothes to a hamper in her room. **Preschooler:** Have her put her clothes in a hamper in the laundry room or sort them into bins. **Child:** Have her help sort clean socks, fold T-shirts, and put away own clothes into drawers or on shelves.
Talks back to parents when told to do something	Does as told, even if unhappy, without backtalk	**Toddler:** Avoid excessively saying no to him. Tell child what you want more often than what you don't want. **Preschooler:** Politely correct inappropriate comments. Teach child how to express negative emotions in an acceptable way. **Child:** Immediately address every episode of backtalk. Define behaviors that aren't permitted. Be consistent.

Typical Older Child/Teenager Misbehavior	Preferred Behavior	How to Help Your Young Child Develop the Preferred Behavior
Ignores parents' requests	Acknowledges a request and does as asked	**Toddler:** Make requests simple, clear, and appropriate to his age. **Preschooler:** Make requests from eye-to-eye level that are clear and specific. **Child:** Follow through with an action (such as taking a child by the hand) if he doesn't respond right away.
Forgets to do chores, such as taking out the trash	Does daily chores without being asked	**Toddler:** Have him help to clean up after self, making it an enjoyable process. **Preschooler:** Have daily cleanup routines. **Child:** Give him specific, daily responsibilities listed on a chore chart.
Bickers and fights with siblings	Gets along with siblings, maturely handling disagreements	**Toddler:** Teach her how to share and how to be kind and gentle to siblings. **Preschooler:** Mediate sibling squabbles and teach them how to solve their own problems. **Child:** Require children to work out their differences while you oversee from a distance.

Typical Older Child/Teenager Misbehavior	Preferred Behavior	How to Help Your Young Child Develop the Preferred Behavior
Shouts or uses foul language	Expresses anger appropriately	**Toddler:** To help her understand herself, acknowledge and label child's emotions. **Preschooler:** Encourage her to talk about her feelings. Help her find resolutions to problems. **Child:** Teach anger management skills, such as taking quiet time alone to cool off.
Treats possessions carelessly	Respects and cares for property	**Toddler:** Don't allow destruction or rough misuse of toys. **Preschooler:** Don't allow too much clutter of unused toys. Don't immediately replace broken toys. **Child:** Don't overindulge. Have child earn some money to buy coveted toys. Keep toys neat and organized.
Is a couch potato, watching too much TV and not getting enough exercise	Watches limited TV, is active, and gets ample exercise	**Toddler:** Limit TV to thirty minutes a day or less. Encourage active games and activities. **Preschooler:** Don't use the TV as a daily babysitter. Make outside play and busy activities the priority. **Child:** Encourage child to participate in sports. Set your home up with plenty of supplies for active play. Limit TV watching time to an agreed-upon amount.

Typical Older Child/Teenager Misbehavior	Preferred Behavior	How to Help Your Young Child Develop the Preferred Behavior
Lies about both big things and small things without concern	Tells the truth, even in difficult situations	**Toddler:** Teach about honesty and model honesty for him. **Preschooler:** Don't punish for mistakes. Coach him to be honest. **Child:** Focus on solutions to problems instead of punishment. Commend his honesty.
Does not communicate with parents	Has open, honest communication with parents	**Toddler:** Play with your child daily. **Preschooler:** Take time daily to listen to her ramblings. Encourage chatter. **Child:** Listen to her, face-to-face and without distraction. Try to see life from her point of view.
Lacks social skills, exhibiting rudeness and thoughtlessness	Is polite and considerate	**Toddler:** Teach good manners. **Preschooler:** Tirelessly and politely remind him to use manners (e.g., saying "please," "thank you," and "excuse me"). **Child:** Model good manners with your child and others. Expect him to use the manners he has been taught.

Building a Strong Foundation

This book is about how to live everyday life with your children in a controlled yet loving and joyous manner. It provides plenty to think about in regard to your role as a parent as well as ways to help you better understand your child. It is filled with practical tips you can use every day to make life easier. However, all these ideas can work so much better when the foundation of your parenting approach is strong and stable.

What creates a strong foundation? What things make a parent calm and confident? What attitudes encourage a child's cooperation? What mind-sets bring about effective, positive discipline? What are the most important concepts for you to learn and use during your child's early years of life? These are important questions with complicated answers.

As I sit here, sending off to college my oldest child, now a lovely young woman, I have been able to look back over the past eighteen years and contemplate the things I've done to help her reach this important milestone. I have asked myself: *What have I learned? What are the most important lessons I should share with parents of young children who are just setting out on the parenting journey?* After much contemplation, I would like to share with you the things I wish someone had told me when I was first starting out as a mother.

The Big Picture Is More Important than Any One Action

From the time your baby is born until the time your child leaves home for college or wherever the future leads, the two of you may

Daddy and Evan, age 2

have more than 100,000 hours to interact and connect. It would be absolutely, utterly impossible for all of those hours to be blissfully happy and precisely choreographed. There will be plenty of rough spots, uncalled-for anger, and mistakes—both on your part and your child's. To even attempt perfection would be ludicrous and stressful, yet as parents most of us criticize ourselves unnecessarily over every negative situation.

Raising a child requires that we make many decisions every single day, from the insignificant to the life-altering. Sometimes it is obvious that you have made the right decision, other times it is unclear, and from time to time it's apparent that you have made a mistake. Nearly every mistake that you make as a parent has been made by a multitude of parents throughout history.

What is more important than any single action is your overall philosophy and approach to raising your child. When love is your foundation, parenting skills are your structure, and your goal is to raise your child to be a good human being with whom you can have a pleasant lifelong relationship, then it is likely things will turn out as you hope.

Contemplate your most important goals for your family and determine which values you will use to guide your decisions. Learn good parenting skills and use them on a daily basis. And then, forgive yourself and your children the mistakes that will inevitably happen along the way.

Relax More and Stress Less

Oh, my! The millions of little things I've stressed about during the past eighteen years! Messy rooms, dirty faces, lost toys, peas not eaten. Not a single one of these things means anything today. Those insignificant, trivial details certainly make up a large part of life, but when they cause a disproportionate amount of angst they conceal the many little joys that children bring into our lives.

View the little things for what they are—little things—and don't let them get in the way of taking pleasure out of every single day of family life.

Mother-Speak

"I always say 'appreciate every step of the way.' Don't look ahead and wish the children were older and in school, or out of school and independent. Don't look behind and be sad over the fact that they grew up so quickly. Just enjoy the moment. Every stage has its pros and cons. No stage is perfect, and every stage passes eventually."

—Bonnie, mother to Ariella, age 16; Yonina, age 14; Dovi, age 12; Mordechai, age 10; Yedidya, age 6; and Liora, age 2

Enjoy the Play More

Be willing to join your little ones in their incredibly enchanting play a little bit more often. You don't always have to have one eye on the clock when you're immersed in playtime with your child. Let the answering machine pick up a few more messages. Ignore the *ding* of incoming e-mail messages on your computer until the fort is complete, the clay zoo is built, or the book is finished.

Mother-Speak

"I was trying to finish all my errands today and clean my house. As I was trying to mop the kitchen floor, my daughter kept standing right in front of me, making it impossible. I tried to explain to her that Mommy needed to mop. I tried to distract her with a toy and take her to another room to play, but she just kept coming right back. So finally I decided the dirty floor wasn't that important and sat down with her on the floor to read a book with her. After a few more books, she went off contentedly to play on her own and I finished the floor.

"Your comment about not watching the clock while you play with your child made me think of myself, obstinately trying to mop the kitchen floor while my little girl stood right in front of me making it impossible. Giving her the little bit of attention she needed *right then*, not waiting until it was convenient for me, removed her as a physical obstacle to my mopping job. But more important, it changed her in my mind from an obstacle into a little person who really needed her mommy to be with her for just a few moments."

—Sarah, mother to Axa, age 2

Of course you play with your children, but far too often you probably feel guilty for that playtime—something "more important" is waiting to be done. If you were to make a list of all those oh-so-important things that have interfered with playtime in the past, I'm sure the list would appear just a little bit foolish now. The important things all got done, I'm sure, although you probably can't remember them all. And I'm certain that a bit more playtime wouldn't have caused chaos. And once your child is a busy teen or a young adult moving out of your home, you'll realize that the most important thing of all was that playtime spent with your child.

Parent and child playtime *is* important. Not only for building children's skills and knowledge of life, but for building relationships between parent and child, too. So, plan for, carry out, and enjoy more playtime with your children. They won't be little forever, you know, and you won't regret the time you spent with them.

Give Yourself More Credit for What You Do Right and Don't Examine So Intently the Things You Do Wrong

We all make mistakes and life is never perfect. Even when we *don't* use our parenting skills, even when we are too stressed, and even when we don't take enough time for playtime, life is usually plenty good enough because we're probably doing more things right than we realize. Family bonds truly can fill in any gaps with a love that transcends mistakes. A caring heart and a warm embrace can make up for less-than-perfect moments. And if you try to be a good parent, the odds are definitely in your favor that you will succeed.

Dedicated parents read parenting books, so I know that if you are reading these words you are a parent who truly cares about doing the best job you can. I also know that the more you read and the more you learn, the more self-critical you may become. It would take a God-like superhuman being to put into practice every single idea that you learn, every moment of every day. The fact that you learn, and do your best to apply what you learn, is commendable.

Do your best, learn from your mistakes, and appreciate that you are doing a grand and important job. Give yourself a pat on the back, and give credit where credit is due. You are doing a better job than you think.

Mother-Speak

"Why do we mothers all feel compelled to be Supermom and then feel let down when we can't do it all?"

—Romi, mother to Carter, age 4, and Brinley, age 19 months

Let Your Heart Win Out Over Voices of Insistent, Insensitive, and Unwanted Advice

When it comes to child-rearing, nearly everyone has an opinion and most people adamantly defend their own beliefs. Not only that, but many people judge other approaches harshly. They often feel compelled to convert others to their way of thinking.

Make decisions about how you want to raise your children. Read books that align with your beliefs, and spend time with other parents who think as you do. Be open to new ideas, but sift them through your moral strainer before you apply them to your own family. Once you make thoughtful decisions, move forward with confidence.

Be Willing to Break the Rules

Throw caution to the wind and follow your heart more often. Cherish every single moment with your children—even the not-so-perfect ones. Loosen up a bit and know that you don't have to be the serious, dull, authoritative boss every single moment of every single day.

Maybe this comes from my experience (raising four children), maybe it comes from being an older mother (age fifty is within striking distance), or maybe it comes from the confidence of being viewed as a parenting expert. Probably it's a combination of all these things, but I have learned to let my hair down a lot more often.

Lately I've been brave a little more often and have risked breaking the rules in favor of good, old-fashioned family bonding. I've taken my teenagers to rock concerts that end at midnight—on a school night. I've let my six-year-old join me in my bed in the middle of the night (and enjoyed every single snuggle). I've let the kids order pizza when no one feels like cooking and eat dessert before dinner so the ice cream won't melt. There's something almost decadent about purposely going against the norm. And there's something very fulfilling about doing it anyway, when it's definitely the right thing to do for your family at that moment.

Of course I don't break every rule, and the ones I selectively break I don't do so every time. But when my heart says *yes*, I'm willing to be a little bit less of a stuffy grown-up and more of a carefree kid. And everyone benefits from that.

If I Had My Child to Raise Over Again
   by Diana Loomans
If I had my child to raise all over again,
I'd finger paint more, and point the finger less.
I'd do less correcting, and more connecting.
I'd take my eyes off my watch, and watch with my eyes.
I would care to know less, and know to care more.
I'd take more hikes and fly more kites.
I'd stop playing serious, and seriously play.
I would run through more fields and gaze at more stars.
I'd do more hugging, and less tugging.
I would be firm less often, and affirm much more.
I'd build self-esteem first, and the house later.
I'd teach less about the love of power,
And more about the power of love.

—From *100 Ways to Build Self-Esteem and Teach Values.*
Copyright 1994, 2003 by Diana Loomans.
Reprinted with permission of H J Kramer/New World
Library, Novato, CA; newworldlibrary.com.

See the World Through Your Child's Eyes

Children are . . . childish. Their actions, thoughts, and words originate in a place of innocence and from an egocentric understanding of the world. If a child wants a cookie, he is thinking only of the rich taste of chocolate and the pleasure it will bring him. He's not thinking about how it affects his appetite for lunch, how it fits into his overall diet, or how the cost fits into the family grocery budget. He's not even thinking if asking fifteen times will make his mother mad. He purely and simply wants a cookie.

If we can avoid evaluating our child's motivation from an adult perspective, but rather view his behavior at face value—as an innocent and undiluted need or want—it will help us choose how to respond in the most effective ways. It will prevent tears and anger—from both you and your child.

Remember that your child is a child and has a lot to learn about life. Keep in mind that he isn't out to get you, he isn't trying to anger you, and he doesn't have a master plan to drive you crazy. He's just going about life in his blissful little world.

Discipline Doesn't Have to Be Unpleasant to Be Effective

There are times when our children teach us more about parenting than any expert documents and research that we could study. One such moment of insight recently occurred for me. I was walking down a busy street with my son, Coleton. As typical of a kindergartener, he was curious about every leaf and bug along the way and he kept lagging behind. Being in a hurry (as we adults too often are) and being concerned about Coleton wandering off, I shouted at him to keep up and quit dawdling. He did catch up with me and, with tear-filled eyes, said, "Next time you feel like being mad at me, why don't you just hug me instead and then tell me what you want me to do." So, we did hug, I explained that he needed to stay close, and we held hands and continued on our way.

Don't be too quick to jump into unforgiving or harsh discipline. Try the gentle methods first—kind requests, polite appeals, and, as Coleton recommends, a hug.

Know That It's Not That Important

What's not that important? Well . . . *nearly everything*. The majority of the annoyances we suffer with our children are due to minor

Ethan, age 3½

issues—whining about bedtime, fussing about sharing a toy, refus-ing to eat a green bean. For the first six or more years of a child's life I can't really think of a single thing that child could do that would truly warrant a parent's anger. Yes, of course we get angry at our children, we are human. But what I'm trying to say is that a young child is incapable of doing anything that would signifi-cantly affect us—the things that they do to push our buttons are inconsequential to the grand picture of life. If we could somehow get through our days with this concept in mind, we parents would be happier and calmer.

Keep your priorities clear. Life will be more peaceful when you can convince yourself that a green bean is only a green bean—not an attack on your values, your parenting skills, or your domestic talents.

Give the Small Stuff Small Attention and the Big Stuff Big Attention

I remember a professor in college telling the class on the very first day, "If you put the same amount of attention into sharpening your pencil as into writing your thesis, you will only succeed in making yourself a nervous wreck." As a parent, you must deal with a million details every single day of life. If you make everything equal on the scale of importance—from putting toys in the toy box to choosing the right preschool, you will very likely make yourself a nervous wreck.

If you can truly manage to give the small things small attention and the big things big attention, you will not only be happier and calmer—your *children* will likely be happier, calmer, and better behaved. Why? Children (and all human beings) have a limited amount of capacity. If your child is attempting to master and respond to an endless amount of parental expectations, then most certainly some will fall through the cracks. If you give the same amount of energy to all things, then you cannot control which things work—and which fail. So, in response to your intense expectations on all fronts, your child might master putting his toys in the toy box when he's done playing but push his baby sister over and step on the dog on his way to get there.

As you move through your days with your child, know that everything cannot be perfect, and your child will not obey all the rules. So make choices, let the little stuff go for later (or for good), and choose your "big stuff" wisely.

Rest Assured That Your Kids Love You, Even When They Hate You (Because They Really Don't)

Raising children requires that you act like a grown-up—that you must tell them *no* when they want to hear *yes* or tell them *stop* when they want to hear *go*. Many such decisions are for your child's safety, many are for her own good, and some are for your own good. I have yet to meet a child capable of understanding adult decisions and responding to being told no or stop with a cheerful, "Good for you, Mommy! Excellent parenting decision."

Remember that children are egocentric—they are concerned primarily with their own needs and wants. Saying no gets in the way of them doing what they want to do. So, they get upset. Their response may be anger, tantrums, or tears, and you may get the feeling that they hate you. But they aren't even thinking about *you*—they are thinking about the thing they want to do but can't. You just happen to be the bearer of bad news.

Know that your child's unhappiness about your decisions and his tears or anger when he is disciplined are normal and natural and not truly directed at you. While your child may not thank

Key Point
Your most important goal as a parent is *not* to make your child happy every minute of every day—that would be easy: providing an endless supply of candy and ice cream and saying yes to every request. Your actual goal is much harder: raise a first-rate human being.

you for your good decisions now (or ever), those decisions are an important part of everyday life and the development of your child as a good human being.

Relax, Because When You're Prepared for the Worst, It Almost Never Happens

Part of the parenting job description is to worry. With our babies we worry about little things such as diaper rash as well as much bigger things such as sudden infant death syndrome. With our toddlers we worry about everything from bruised knees to delays in developmental milestones. As our children grow, so do our worries.

Worry itself is useless. Studies even tell us that most of the things we worry about never happen. It is better to be prepared and knowledgeable and then, to state it very simply, *don't think about it so much.* Banish needless worry—it's a waste of a good imagination.

When the Worst Does Happen, You'll Get Through It and You'll Move On

Bad things do happen. Some things we have no control over, and some are a result of decisions made. But either way, when bad things happen, we cannot manipulate time and make them not happen. What we can do, however, is adjust how we think and what we do and move past even the most difficult situations. In all but the most extreme cases, we, as human beings, are resilient and adaptable.

When difficult situations arise take time to analyze them. Talk to others. Read books. Make a plan for how you will handle things. And then proceed to carry out your plan.

Live in the Moment

A parent's job is complicated and time-consuming. Add on the countless other tasks that fill up our days, and it is a never-ending process of juggling too many balls. One of the biggest problems comes from not only handling the balls in your hands, but looking at and thinking about all the other balls that are still up in the air. As you're busy looking at them, the ones in your hands suffer because they never get your full attention.

Let's take a practical example. Think of the times you sit on the floor playing with your child. Not being in the moment is when you are watching the clock, worrying about other things you must do, or feeling bored with children's games. Being in the moment is choosing to truly connect and enjoy your child—even if it's only for ten minutes—watching her mouth form words as she speaks, watching her hands as she expresses her ideas, enjoying the enthusiasm of her imagination, listening to her ideas, absorbing what she believes, and cherishing the little person that she is.

The added beauty of being in the moment is that your child will feel the difference. Having a distracted Mommy or Daddy sitting beside her on the floor as she plays feels very different than having the same parent engaged and absorbing the beauty of the moment. And it is the combination of many such moments that builds a relationship.

The more that you can embrace living in the moment as a part of who you are, the more fulfilling your everyday life will be.

Discipline and Emotional Control

Take a moment to think about how you respond to emotionally challenging situations in your own life.

- When you and your spouse have a disagreement, do you always respond with a calm, purposeful explanation of your position?
- When your mother-in-law gives you unwanted advice, do you cheerfully thank her for her kind wisdom (and then call your best friend to rave about her thoughtfulness)?
- When your child spills chocolate milk on the living room rug, do you joyfully whistle while you apply rug cleaner?
- When you delete the wrong computer file or burn dinner or when the dog has an accident on the carpet, do you smile and cheerfully announce, "No problem! That's life!"?

While I am sure there are times your response to emotional situations such as these is calm and pleasant, I suspect that far too frequently your reaction is annoyance, anger, impatience, and maybe even an adult-sized temper tantrum. The human experience involves facing numerous challenges, yet we don't always have the patience, understanding, or restraint to respond in the best possible way.

So, here's the million dollar question: *If we capable, mature adults cannot control our emotions completely, is it even remotely possible that our children would be capable of such a feat?*

Is it possible that this lack of emotional control is at the root of young children's negative behaviors? Is it possible that misbehavior is the symptom, but the real problem is immaturity? Look at the following list of the most common childish misbehaviors and check whether you think these could be caused by a lack of emotional control—an inability to handle strong emotions such as frustration, anger, and powerlessness.

Behavior

Could be caused by a lack of emotional control?	YES	NO
Backtalk	____	____
Biting a playmate	____	____
Clinging	____	____
Crying	____	____
Hitting a parent	____	____
Impatience	____	____
Interrupting	____	____
Kicking a sibling	____	____
Screaming and yelling	____	____
Separation anxiety	____	____
Squabbles over sharing	____	____
Stubbornness	____	____
Teasing	____	____
Temper tantrums	____	____
Whining and fussing	____	____

Are you a bit surprised that ALL of the most common childish misbehaviors are likely caused by a child's undeveloped emotional control? Yes, *all* of them! Every single one! Is it possible that any child on the face of this earth could be born with mature understanding and emotional control? No, of course it is not. Even the smartest, sweetest, most peaceful child could not possibly be born with the wisdom and ability to totally control his or her emotions. (And let's not forget that adults don't even possess this gift.)

So what does this mean for you and your view of your child's actions? You now have the key to understanding your child's mis-

Father-Speak

"We have an old Irish saying that I use when one of my girls is hollering or fussing: 'You'll be better before you're married.' It doesn't offer much comfort to the child, of course, but it does help the grown-ups! All these little trials will pass and someday be forgotten. It's a philosophy that puts the end goal in perspective. The point is getting them safely and sanely to adulthood."

—Raymond, father to Elena, age 4, and Eva, age 2

behavior in a way that can allow you to gently discipline in the context of the true meaning of the word: to teach and to lead.

The next time your child misbehaves by having a temper tantrum, hitting a friend, or yelling at you—instead of looking at him and thinking *What a brat!*, you can instead think, *Whoa. This child is seriously lacking emotional control.* You can step back, calm down, and understand that it's not a lack of parenting skills and it's not a defect in your child's personality, it's just ordinary human growth.

The Most Important Concept to Remember

Your child doesn't whine, fuss, and have temper tantrums because she is trying to manipulate you. She isn't purposely being "bad." She doesn't misbehave just to make you angry. Your child's misbehaviors are a direct result of the fact that she cannot control her emotions. This is biologically, psychologically, and absolutely normal.

Key Point

A child is emotion in motion—untamed emotion in constant motion. Only with maturity and experience will a child develop the tools that bring emotional control.

If you can keep this one vital fact in the forefront of your mind, I guarantee that the next eighteen or so years will be much happier and immeasurably more peaceful for you. It will also give you the presence of mind to help your child learn how to develop appropriate emotional control.

The Four Parts
to Discipline

Discipline is a very complicated and complex matter. We want to enjoy our children, we don't want to stress about the little things, and we want to be forgiving to our children and ourselves. However, there are many, many things we must get our children to do or stop from doing. There are lots of daily tasks that must be completed. And children don't always listen, they don't always do the things we want them to do, and they have a limited amount of knowledge and emotional control. As I see it, there are four distinct parts to the purpose and goal of discipline.

1. To correct immediate behavior
2. To teach a lesson
3. To give tools that build self-discipline and emotional control
4. To build the parent/child relationship

Let's examine how these parts apply to a few typical situations so that you can begin to understand how these four purposes color almost every discipline situation with your child.

Situation: Your child is having a temper tantrum in a store because you won't buy a new toy.

1. **Correct immediate behavior.** Take your child to a restroom or unpopulated corner of the store. Wait for your child to stop the tantrum.
2. **Teach a lesson.** You can't have everything you want. You need to express your emotions appropriately.

3. **Give tools to build self-discipline and emotional control.** Help your child write a list of toys that she wants but can't have right now.
4. **Build the relationship.** Demonstrate leadership, understanding, and patience.

Situation: Your two children are squabbling over a toy.

1. **Correct immediate behavior.** Put the toy on the counter while you get your children to stop tussling and pay attention to you.
2. **Teach a lesson.** Children need to learn how to share toys and take turns.
3. **Give tools to build self-discipline and emotional control.** Help children by setting a timer so each can have a five-minute turn playing with the toy. Show them how to do this in the future without your help.
4. **Build the relationship.** Show them how to play together and how to settle disputes. Show them that they can look to you for help in handling problems.

Situation: Your child is upset with a playmate and bites her on the arm.

1. **Correct immediate behavior.** Separate the children. Provide attention and care to the child who was bitten.
2. **Teach a lesson.** Get down to your child's level, put your hands on her shoulders, look her in the eye, and say, "Biting hurts. We don't bite. Offer Emmy a hug. That might make her feel better."
3. **Give tools to build self-discipline and emotional control.** Give your child a few hints on how she should handle her frustration next time. "If you want a toy, you can ask nicely for it or you can come to Mommy for help."

4. **Build the relationship.** Show your child that you are on her side even when she makes mistakes. Demonstrate that she can count on you to teach her how to handle strong emotions.

Discipline Is Not a One-Time Maneuver

You say you've tried to get your little one to put his toys away, but he never does. You're after your daughter constantly not to whine, yet that screechy voice continues. You repeatedly attempt to get your two children to share their toys *nicely*, yet it seems that daily you're refereeing an argument. No matter what you do, the same issues keep coming up over and over again.

Arianna, age 2

Think about something that you do or don't do—but that you know you should do differently. Perhaps it's exercising or eating healthily. Maybe it's keeping your desk organized or your closet clean. Perhaps it's staying calm when your flight is delayed or you are stuck in traffic. In all of these examples it's likely that you struggle to always do the right thing, even when you know what the right thing is. So, if you, the mature adult, still don't do everything the right way, how can you possibly expect such a feat from your young child?

Discipline means to teach—and it is a very rare lesson that can be learned in one simple session. Furthermore, young children cannot easily apply what they've learned in one situation to another. So even minor variations create entirely new scenarios— for example, learning to share toys with a sibling at home isn't easily transposed to sharing playground equipment with a friend at the park.

> **Mother-Speak**
> "Too often we are caught saying, 'How many times have I said . . . ?' We forget that children *need* repetitive teaching to learn."
> **—Sonja, mother to Ekatarina, age 3, and Aleksandar, age 1**

What this all means is that you must teach the same, or similar, lessons over and over and over and *over* again in many different ways until, perhaps, your child will master the idea and claim it as his own. Even then, just because a child knows what is right doesn't mean he will always do the right thing. (Do you *always* drive the posted speed limit?) Our job as parents is to help our children learn right from wrong and how to make the right decisions in life. It is to guide and teach our children, every day, in many ways.

Discipline means teaching, and as such it can encompass almost every interaction you have with your child. When you are thoughtful about your role as a parent, keep your eye on long-term goals, and use carefully planned parenting skills, then your essential parenting attitudes will be properly aligned. That's when you will avoid confrontation and tears, and your job as a parent will be much more fulfilling and rewarding.

Part 2

No-Cry Discipline Parenting
Skills and Tools

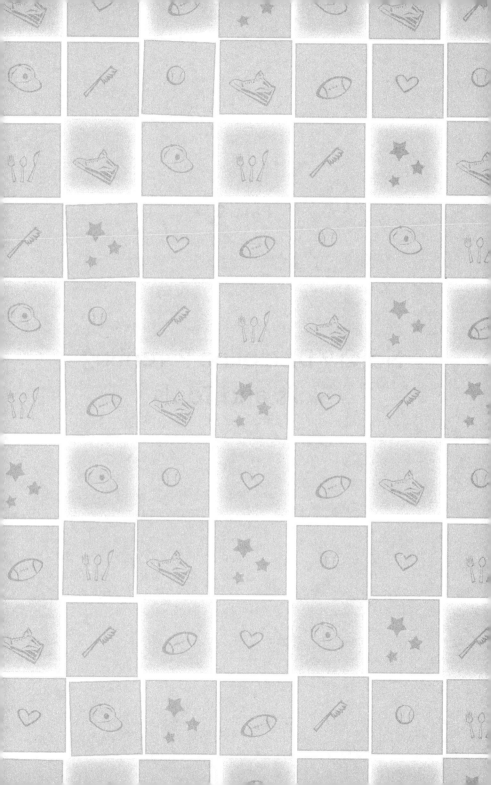

Everyday Challenges

Children are joy. We love them with every cell of our being, and we can't imagine what our world would be like without them. Yet, everyday life with our children can be challenging, frustrating, and exhausting. All day, every day, there are so many things we must get our children to do—or stop from doing. Beginning with getting them out of bed in the morning, and ending with putting them to bed at night (and maybe not even then), a parent's job involves providing an incredible amount of organization, guidance, direction, and correction. Regardless of our beliefs about parenting, our theories about children, or our life goals, it is the essence of everyday living—the daily routines and ordinary actions—that make up life.

When you have young children in your home, this everyday life can be a challenging adventure from sunup to sundown. Even when you try to see the big picture and make decisions based on your goals for the future, the daily process of living seems to create a whirlwind of activity and emotions so that in any given moment your thoughts are wholly focused on the *now*. This is very different from living in the moment and enjoying it. Instead, we often struggle through the day, trying to stay ahead of the many problems and frustrations that arise. You may *want* to focus your decisions on creating joy, achieving your goals, and seeing the big picture of your child's future, but you can't even begin to see that big picture because there are so many little pictures in the way. Who would have ever thought that simple tasks, such as putting on shoes, brushing teeth, or giving a bath would require so much preparation, negotiation, and emotion? And who would have thought that raising one tiny child could bring so many frustrating everyday challenges?

Father-Speak

"I didn't think for an instant that raising children would be easy, but I also didn't think it would be the emotional roller coaster that it has been."

—Alan, father to Leanne, age 3, and Timothy, age 5 months

Here's the good news: There are very specific approaches that work wonders to keep you calm and in control, help you make good long-term decisions, and help you encourage your child to *willingly* cooperate with you. Using these methods will help your day run more smoothly, and they will help you build a close, loving relationship with your children that can last a lifetime. These methods also will allow you to live in the joy of the moment, since you won't be immersed in the juggling of all those issues involved in daily survival.

A special side effect of using these approaches is that they will actually prevent many of the tantrums, battles, and tears that can spoil your day. By using these methods you are using *preventive discipline*. And the more consistent you are in using these approaches, the better your child's daily behavior will be. Looking even farther down the road, your child will more likely have solid self-discipline patterns for the future.

Key Point

You would be stunned to know how many negative behaviors you actually prevent from happening when you improve the way you interact with your child.

Miriam, age 4; Moshe, age 3; and Raizel, age 4

Keep in mind that as children grow they change. Certain skills that work beautifully with toddlers often fall flat with preschoolers and only cause eye-rolling with older children. Some approaches will work every single time with one child, yet never work at all with his or her brother. In addition, parents are as different from one another as children are, so some of the methods will work perfectly for one parent and fail miserably for the other. It takes some experimentation to figure out what works best for you and your family. But once you settle on a few specific ideas, you'll feel more confident and your home will be more peaceful. You'll establish routines and patterns that will allow you to make better short- and long-term decisions over the next eighteen or more years.

Read through the techniques that follow, and think about the various no-cry discipline methods that are described. You'll see that there is no one method prescribed for all families because every family is different and discipline tools should never be one-size-fits-all. The beauty of having various options to choose from is that by selecting those that fit each particular parent/child pair best, you can avoid the frustration and tears that result when parents attempt to follow an outsider's advice about what is best for them. You know yourself and your child, so choose the ideas that appeal to you, try them out, and gauge the results. Practice and refine as you go. Eventually you'll find your own comfortable rhythm and you'll feel more confident and capable. Revisit this book from time to time to fine-tune your actions, adjust them to your growing child, and remind yourself of your goals. This active style of parenting will make your parenting journey more joyful as well as keep you on track to meet your long-term goals for your child.

First, Solve the Real Problem

Often, when a child is stubborn, has a tantrum, fights with a sibling, whines, cries, or dawdles, the issue that sets off the behavior has little to do with anything that requires an act of discipline by the parent. Just as adults who are experiencing a bad day, a bad mood, a headache, or some other personal issue might snap at a spouse, yell at a child, or "kick the cat," children may be struggling with emotions or situations that cause them to respond as they do. Responding to a child's actions with knee-jerk discipline often escalates the tantrum or tears. The problem will not be addressed, and the lesson will not be learned. In essence, the issue then is *not* always about how to discipline children but how to change the environment in order to help them gain control over their emotions and reactions. By changing the environment you can help a child calm himself down, thus opening the door to a true learning experience.

In the following pages are some of the most common problems that cause children to act out in negative ways, as well as some solutions to guide you as you try to help your child cope. These are all preventive, proactive, no-cry discipline processes, and they may even help you prevent negative behavior.

The Problem: Tiredness

How much and how well a child sleeps has a role in *everything* from dawdling, crankiness, temper tantrums, and hyperactivity to physical growth, overall health, and the ability to learn to tie his or her shoes and recite the alphabet. *Everything.* A sleep study completed at Tel Aviv University demonstrated that even a one-hour shortage in appropriate sleep time compromises a child's behavior. Missed naps, bedtimes that are too late, night wakings, or early risings can cause unpleasant changes in your child's daytime behavior.

This issue is further complicated because when children aren't sleeping, Mom and Dad aren't sleeping either. We simply cannot function well as parents—or, as a matter of fact, as people—when our own sleep is continually disturbed. We become fatigued, and our responses to our child's misbehavior are less than stellar. Instead of using skills that gain control of the situation, a sleep-deprived parent lacks patience and tries to force changes, often leading to meltdowns on both sides.

Mother-Speak

"I notice that Matthew misbehaves the most when he is tired. If he only naps for an hour instead of his usual two-hour nap, he tends to be fussy and clingy. And if he hasn't had a nap at all, he will start to hit or throw things. When he doesn't nap, it causes unnecessary misbehaviors and frustration. So now I do my best to try to let him have a nap, even if we are on the go, because in the long run it is better for everyone."

—Genevieve, mother to Matthew, age 2

Solutions

Make the effort to solve any sleep issues—both night sleep and nap time. If your child is five years old or younger, plan for a daily nap. You can't force a child to sleep, of course, but you can set up a situation that invites relaxation and encourages sleep. A good time for a nap is soon after lunch. Create a post-lunch routine where your child lies in a dark room and listens to music or an audio book. If your child is tired, he should fall asleep easily under these conditions, and if he doesn't sleep the rest time will still be good for him.

If your child isn't sleeping well at night, do whatever you can to solve the problem. A few quick tips that may get you started on the right path include:

- Aim for an early bedtime.
- Dim the lights and calm the activity the hour before that bedtime.
- Have a pleasant, relaxing pre-bed routine.
- Have your child go to bed at the same time seven days a week.

If you are struggling with sleep issues, there is more specific help for you in Part 4, Specific Solutions for Everyday Problems, as well as in my books *The No-Cry Sleep Solution* and *The No-Cry Sleep Solution for Toddlers and Preschoolers*.

The Problem: Hunger

Children can't always identify feelings of hunger, yet being hungry can negatively affect their energy, mood, stamina, and ability to focus and concentrate. While adults have learned how to identify and cope with hunger, children have years to go before they develop this ability, so even mild hunger can trip them up.

Children can also be adversely affected by poor food choices that don't adequately fuel their bodies with proper nutrition. Your child may be drawn to carbohydrates, as many are—toast or cereal for breakfast, macaroni for lunch, crackers for a snack, and potatoes for dinner. Sadly lacking are protein, fruits, and vegetables. An unbalanced diet such as this can directly affect your child's moods, health, digestion, and elimination. Children can become

Aanyah, age 2

uncomfortable, unpleasant, and lagging in energy without understanding that a healthy snack or meal would help them feel much
better.

Solutions

It's best to provide your child with breakfast (soon after he or
she wakes in the morning), lunch, and dinner plus two or three

healthy snacks (between the meals) every day. Children don't need big meals, but they do need frequent nourishment to stabilize their behavior.

In addition to regular meals and snacks, take a good look at the kinds of food your child is eating. Is your child's diet healthy and balanced? Does it contain choices from all the food groups? The composition of your child's meal will determine how it affects behavior and for how long. Balanced meals that contain healthy choices from a variety of food groups will have a much better impact than a snack consisting of only one type of food. When that one food is a nonnutritious choice, such as French fries or cookies, the impact on your child's mood will be only marginally better than the hunger it replaces. A high-nutrition meal or snack can refuel your child and improve behavior.

Children who have undetected food sensitivities or food allergies may have related behavior problems. Signs of a food-related allergy can appear soon after a child eats the food or several hours later. The most common signs are diarrhea, vomiting, abdominal pain, wheezing, coughing, rash, fussiness, gassiness, and difficulty sleeping. Your child may have only one or two of these symptoms. If you suspect that your child may have a food allergy, talk to a medical professional.

Father-Speak

"I am always surprised to see how some parents' lifestyles have become so busy that they don't notice the signals that their children are sending to them. It often ends in frustration for both the parent and the child, when the issue could have been easily avoided."

—Ole, father to Lucas, age 3

Improving your child's diet is a simple idea with a big pay-off. Make an effort to provide many small servings of a variety of healthy foods each day to prevent hunger-based behavior problems.

The Problem: Frustration

Children's minds are often one step ahead of their physical abilities. They may want to tie their shoes and they may think they know how to tie their shoes, but when they grasp those laces they just can't get them to tie! In their frustration—and their desire to succeed—they often get discouraged and angry. They desperately want to succeed, and, as nature would dictate, they are determined to keep trying even when they fail repeatedly—which often makes them appear to be unreasonable and stubborn.

While we do want our children to learn how to be independent, we don't always have time for the learning process nor do we always identify this as the cause of stubborn behavior, so our own impatience makes our children dig in their heels even deeper. This, of course, makes us even more upset, and so goes around the circle of negative emotions.

Solutions

Understand that your child has a biological drive to master her world, yet oftentimes she's unable to achieve the things she sets out to do.

There are times when you can allow your child plenty of time to practice a new skill. Other times, when you are in a hurry or when your child is clearly frustrated, there's no rule against helping your child accomplish any task.

Mother-Speak

"My daughter has suddenly become very independent. She decided that it was time to learn how to dress herself. My normally quiet, even-tempered toddler was now yelling, groaning, grunting, and at times crying in her room. And this didn't just occur in the morning—oh no, we had to experience five or six clothing changes every day. At first I was annoyed with her frustrated attempts, and yet she wouldn't accept help. I determined that the easiest way to handle the aggravation was to allow plenty of time for clothing changes several times a day. I let go of the need to control her cute outfits and perfect hair and just let her wear anything she could get her hands on. Inside, outside, all around the house and neighborhood she proudly displayed her unique clothing accomplishments. Two weeks later, I have to say that my willingness to give her space and time, and give up my own agenda, has paid off. She's now down to only two outfits a day in less than five minutes each! Proof that practice makes perfect, even if Mama has to put up with some toddler-style frustration!"

—**Sarah, mother to Gracie, age 3, and Sam, age 1**

Yes, we want to teach our children to be independent, but we don't need to do it all in one day. Sometimes, it's better for you to take over and save the practice for later, during a calmer moment. When you do have the time, a few minutes of guidance and direction can go a long way toward helping your child learn to master a task. You may also want to look for opportunities to help your child practice her many new skills under unrushed circumstances.

Mother-Speak

"I have had to tell my child, 'It's okay for Mommy to help you.' He wants so badly to do it by himself that although he is having trouble, he refuses help. I think letting him know that accepting help is okay helps him relax."

—Stacey, mother to Tasneem, age 7; Umar, age 5; Yusuf, age 2; and Zayd, age 1

The Problem: Boredom

Children are incredibly curious and on a constant quest for knowledge. It is a biological necessity and is as powerful a need as hunger or thirst. A child's job is to learn new things, and when we don't provide the proper stimulus, he will find it himself, or fill the void with an emotional breakdown. For example, if your child is ushered around town for hours as you run countless mundane errands, it's likely a tantrum and fussiness will be going right along with you. If he is put in the same room and given the same toys day after day to occupy his time, his boredom with the unchanging environment will often lead him to search for stimulation and experiment in ways that are perceived as misbehavior.

Solutions

Quench your child's never-ending thirst for learning something new—no matter where you are. When you're on the go, bring along a small bag of toys, books, and snacks. Point out interesting things at your destinations. Play word games. "I spy something red." "How many things can you find that start with the letter B?" "What word rhymes with cat?" "Can you count the people standing in line?"

A great boredom buster is to get your child involved in what you are doing. Even a toddler can pick three red apples at the grocery store, snap peas in half during dinner preparation, and fetch a diaper when you are changing the baby. Children who are actively involved and engaged tend to be happier and less disruptive than those who are bored and unfocused.

Rotate the toys that are available to your child for playtime—separate your child's toys into three boxes and put out one-third at a time in his play area. Every few days, or once a week, rotate the boxes to keep the offerings fresh. Add new things to the mix often. Avoid noncreative toys with limited purpose. Instead search for toys that have long play value and that can be used in a variety of ways, such as building blocks, toy animals, and miniatures of real-life things (play kitchen sets or tools, for example).

Frequently a daily routine involves having a child play in exactly the same place day after day—often in a toy corner. I encourage you to set up various small play centers throughout your house, since a new environment provides interesting changes and will keep a child happy and engaged much longer.

Here's one more thing to keep in mind: while you want to provide your child with the tools to stay busy and interested, you don't want to become the tour director. Give your child toys and direction, but don't feel that you must orchestrate every activity. Nor should you be the permanent playmate. Encourage your child's ability for independent play.

The Problem: Overstimulation

Certain types of situations are breeding grounds for children's unruly behavior. When a child or a group of children are in an intense, noisy, active situation there is a good chance their behavior will also be intense, noisy, and active. Typical situations

Arianna, age 2½; Kailee, age 4; and Ellianna, age 2½

involve birthday parties, family gatherings, playgrounds, carnivals, and shopping malls. Children take in all the sights, sounds, and motion around them, and it seems that they cannot sift through it all, so everything at once is absorbed right into their actions. Wanting to take it all in and do everything that can be done, they become a reflection of the commotion surrounding them.

Solutions

First, be prepared in advance. Your child shouldn't arrive tired or hungry. Try to plan the schedule so it doesn't interfere with usual nap times or mealtimes. If the excursion is to be more than an hour long, plan to purchase snacks or bring along a few healthy snacks, such as pretzels and cheese or granola mix, plus something to drink.

Remember that no matter how busy the planned day will be, there will likely be lulls in the activity—such as waiting in line, drives to the destination, or time at the table waiting for food to be served. Have an assortment of small toys, activities, and books with you to fill any waiting spaces.

A verbal preparation lesson can be helpful. Tell your child a story in advance that details exactly what she should expect—where you are going and what you will be doing. This is a great activity to do in the car or bus on the way to your destination.

If you find your child becoming agitated, try to move off to a quiet place for a few minutes, like a bathroom, or go for a walk outside. A quiet hug or cuddle can often calm a child down. Allow your child to relax and regroup before reentering the activity. Remember to watch for signs of tiredness, hunger, or frustration, too.

The Problem: Fear

There are times when children are scared of something but can't communicate their fear. Other times a child may feel his fear is inappropriate, so he shouldn't admit to it. Instead of letting you know he is afraid, a child might whine, dawdle, or fight you, giving you the impression he is just being difficult. Typical situations for this type of fear are bedtime, separation from parents, visits to unfamiliar places, or meeting new people.

Fear can also be present when a child is adjusting to major changes in the family, such as the birth or adoption of a sibling, the parents' divorce or marriage, or a move to a new home. At these times parents may be somewhat emotionally unavailable due to their own busyness or adjustment, leaving a child to struggle with unidentified feelings on his own.

Solutions

Examine your child's actions and environment to determine if fear may be the cause of the behavior. If you think this might be the case, you can begin by casually asking leading questions to find out if you've correctly identified a problem. Avoid questions that invite a yes or no answer; instead ask open-ended questions that invite more discussion. If your child doesn't respond to direct questions, you can use puppets, stuffed animals, or other toys to play-act the situation together. Then pay close attention to what your child's character does or says.

Once you've identified your child's fear, see if you can find ways to help him overcome it. This may involve talking or an action— such as installing a night-light and buying a flashlight to overcome a fear of the dark. Or, it might mean approaching a new situation a bit more slowly and cautiously, such as visiting a new home and neighborhood a few times in advance of your family's move. You can also read books together that show how other children master similar situations.

The Problem: Feeling Powerless

Children have little say or control over their lives. Parents and others tell them what to do and when to do it. While this is often accepted as the way things are, there are times when a child feels very strongly about something but is directed to do the opposite. A typical example is when a child is having a grand time playing at a playground or with a friend and is told that it's time to stop and go home. Other times, we impose an unpleasant task on a child who doesn't understand why we are so adamant that it must be done—brushing teeth, bathing, sharing toys, and eating green vegetables, for instance.

Solutions

There are several approaches that can help to alleviate the feeling of powerlessness that often causes a child to erupt with unpleasant behavior. The first is to simply acknowledge a child's feelings. "I know you are having fun and don't want to go." You can follow this up with the facts. "But the bus leaves soon." Sometimes children feel better just knowing that someone truly understands how they feel.

It can also help to give a child a clear warning of what's to come, so that he is prepared and not caught off guard. "We have to leave in ten minutes." Or give a younger child a gauge that he can understand. "We have time for two more trips down the slide." Once ten minutes have passed, or two more trips down the slide have been accomplished, it's time to leave. If you suddenly strike up a conversation with another parent or get involved in reading your book, then your child will quickly learn that warnings are meaningless—so try to stick with your plan.

Another way to give a child more control over his destiny is to offer a choice. It can lead where you want to go, but with an option along the way. "Do you want to walk to the bus stop or have a race?"

Take advantage of times when you can allow a child more input in some areas of his life. This input can create an investment on your child's part and prevent him from seeing something as an unpleasant surprise. For example, you might ask his input when you are creating the week's dinner menus, bring him along when clothes shopping, or invite him to help you plan the day's errands. Even a tiny bit of involvement can make him feel important and happy about the choices.

The Problem: Confusion

The amount of things that your child has learned in his lifetime is mind-boggling. Your child has learned how to speak and understand an entire language, including names for things, feelings, and concepts. He has figured out his place in the world and how to interact with other people in varied situations. The list of things learned is long, indeed, but it is far, far, *far* from complete. There is a lifetime of new things and concepts to be learned. One of those things is the understanding of just how incomplete his own knowledge really is. Everything your child does is based on this limited understanding of the world and the lack of perception about his limits. This base of limited information is what your child uses to function every day. He applies what he knows to a situation to make decisions, and oftentimes he doesn't have enough background to truly understand what's happening. As a simple example, your child may be skilled at riding a tricycle, but even a master tricyclist won't ride off on his own the first time he rides a bicycle.

Solutions

Your child has been on this earth only a few short years, and it may help you to remember this during his tantrums or meltdowns. He's learning more day by day, and he relies on you for much of his information. Be patient and understanding.

As you have seen, there are many underlying issues that can cause behavior problems. Here are more to add to that list:

- Disappointment
- Embarrassment
- Excitement
- Forgetfulness

- Impatience
- Jealousy
- Pain
- Sadness
- Shame
- Shyness
- Stress

It can help to examine your child's primary emotions and make an attempt to address them when you are faced with misbehavior. This can help you find the most effective responses to correcting your child's behavior. You won't be ineffectively dealing with a symptom (the behavior), you will be addressing the problem at its most basic root (the underlying emotion).

Mother-Speak

"This idea of *solving the real problem* has given me back a feeling of control and intuition that I developed during my first year of raising my baby using attachment parenting. Instead of selfishly thinking *Why is she doing this to me?* or feeling bad when others think she is spoilt or manipulative, I try to find the real problem and attend to it before it reaches the 'critical stage.' When I am successful, I am empowered to point out to my critics that there was a reason for the behavior and how great it is to validate that I actually 'know' my child. This is about approaching discipline with a totally different mind-set, which requires an effort to keep the question consciously in my mind before I react. It brings my parenting skills to a whole new level."

—Sonja, mother to Ekaterina, age 3, and Aleksandar, age 1

There are times, of course, when you simply can't unearth the underlying problem, even though one exists. A child may not have the words to express his or her feelings, and you may be unable to figure out what's going on inside that little head. At those times, a cuddle and a bit of unconditional love and understanding may be helpful.

Discipline and Cooperation
Choose Your Adventure

Convincing a young child to cooperate is a little bit like going on a vacation adventure. You can buy your ticket and set a plan, but you never know what will happen after that. You may end up with a wonderful experience or you may not get at all what you expected. You might even get on the wrong bus and have a totally different trip than you planned!

Each parent has certain ways of getting their child to cooperate, a "bag of tricks" if you will. Some parents have one or two items in their bag—it's like a tiny plastic snack baggie. If they use the one tool they have—a time-out, for example—and it doesn't bring results, they can only get frustrated and angry because they are caught holding an empty bag and standing next to a crying child.

On the other hand, parents who are open to learning and using a variety of methods have a huge laundry bag filled with many different options. They can sift through the contents and use whichever technique seems to be right in any given situation. If one technique doesn't work, it's a simple matter to pick another one from the bag—and continue doing so until the right approach brings the desired results. The additional advantage to this big bag of options is that you are less likely to give in to anger or frustration and resort to ineffective spontaneous reactions that bring about the ear-muffling tears that we are trying to avoid.

Because human beings—children and adults—are complicated beings, there isn't one technique that will work in all situations with all people. Therefore, it's best if you have that great big bag of "parenting tricks" that you can sift through when you need a solution. My goal in this chapter is to fill your bag with plenty of new ideas. You'll want to read through these with a pen in hand and note the ideas that feel right to you. Try them out with your child, and keep those that bring you good results. Keep in mind that it may take a few practice runs before you adapt a skill to your personality and your child's traits, too. And as your child grows and changes, your skill collection will need to change as well.

The Same Yesterday, Today, and Tomorrow: Consistency

Many parents tell me that they are amazed at how well their child cooperates at day care with cleanup time, when the same child never cleans up at home. Many parents are surprised at how their child sits quietly for circle time at preschool but won't sit still for two minutes at home. Parents are shocked that their child is always

Isabella, age 3½; Margaret, age 6; and Madeline, age 7

respectful and polite at school but not at home. There actually is no mystery here. Most day-care centers and preschools have big groups of children, which require extremely consistent routines and discipline in order to run smoothly. The first time children break a rule, they are immediately corrected and reminded of the rule. The children also watch everyone else functioning according to the consistent guidelines of the group. This consistency is often lacking at home, and children figure that out quickly. Without consistent responses to their behavior, they learn they can do whatever they want since there is a good chance no one will stop them.

Think about the important discipline issues in your family— what are they? Whining? Backtalk? Tantrums? Bickering? Then decide how these problems will be handled. Examine the times of day that most often present problems for you. Dinnertime? Bath time? Bedtime? Set a plan for these time periods and then stick to it as much as possible.

No parent can be consistent 100 percent of the time, but the more you can make specific decisions about discipline and then follow through regularly, the easier life will be for you and your children, too.

The Power of Offering Choices

Giving a choice is a very effective tool that can be used with children of all ages. You can offer choices based on your child's age and your intent. A toddler can handle two choices while a grade-school child can handle three or four. Only offer a choice that you would be happy with if your child chooses it.

Here are examples of choices:

Do you want to wear your blue pants or your purple skirt?
What do you want to do first: brush your teeth or put on your pajamas?

Would you like to run to the door or hop like a kangaroo?
Do you want to watch ten more minutes of TV or have ten extra minutes for storytime?

A typical hitch when offering choices is that a child may make up his or her own choice. For example, "Taylor, do you want to put on your pajamas first or brush your teeth?" To which little Taylor answers, "I want to watch TV." What do you do? Just smile sweetly and say, "That wasn't one of the choices. What do you want to do first, put on your pajamas or brush your teeth?"

If your child is still reluctant to choose from the options that you offer, then simply ask, "Would you like to choose or shall I choose for you?" If an appropriate answer is not forthcoming, then you can say, "I see that you want me to choose for you." Then *follow through.* Make your choice and help your child—by leading or carrying him—so that he can cooperate. In this case, shut off the TV and lead him into the bathroom and hand him a toothbrush.

Playing to Win: Cooperation Games

Children see life as one big game—so why not take advantage of that? Nearly any task can be turned into a game with very little effort. Some games can be a one-time fix; others can become part of your regular routine. Look at these situations—first the standard serious parent approach (which often leads to fussing and tantrums) and then the "game" approach. Imagine your child's response to both.

Serious: "Pick up your toys and put them in the toy box."
Game: "I bet I can pick up all the blue cars before you pick up the red ones!"

Serious: "Put your pajamas on—now!"
Game: "I'm going to set the timer for ten minutes. I wonder if you can beat the bell and get your pajamas on before it rings."

> **Mother-Speak**
>
> "One of our favorite techniques is the 'No smiling allowed in this house' game. When one of our gals is in a grumpy mood, they can often be cajoled into a better mood by being told, 'Whatever you do, do not smile.' Ninety-nine percent of the time, this elicits a smile and they move toward a more positive mood—works much better than giving them a lecture about being cranky!"
>
> —**Jan, mother to Madeline, age 7, and Bella, age 3**

Serious: "Eat your vegetables. They're good for you."
Game: "Last time I had a plate full of vegetables, a bunny would eat some every time I turned around and wasn't looking. I couldn't believe it! I wonder if that will happen again?" (Parent makes a big production of turning around so that the "bunny" can steal food.)

Serious: "Drink your milk."
Game: "Don't drink that milk! If you do it will make you really strong and then you'll win when we wrestle. Stop! Don't drink it!"

Serious: "Come on. Walk faster. We need to get home."
Game: "Look at me—I'm a pony! And I'm so fast I bet you can't catch me. . . ."

Serious: "You need to go potty. Put your toy down and go potty now."
Game: "Here comes the potty train. Chooo! Chooo! All aboard for the potty-town stop!"

You certainly don't have to fill every request with fun and games—nor should you. However, this technique is a handy and lighthearted way to get through some of the bumps in your day.

Make It Talk: The Remarkable Works-Every-Time Performance

Toddlers and preschoolers require finesse to gain their cooperation. They have not yet reached the age at which they can see and understand the whole picture, so simply explaining what you want doesn't always work. Robert Scotellaro is quoted in *The Funny Side of Parenthood* as saying, "Reasoning with a two-year-old is about as productive as changing seats on the *Titanic*." (He must have had a two-year-old at the time he said this.)

You can get around this frustrating state of affairs by changing your approach. Let's look at two situations—first the typical ("*Titanic*") way:

Parent: Ryan! Time to change your diaper.

Ryan: No! (As he runs off)

Parent: Come on, honey. It's time to leave. I need to change you.

Ryan: (Giggles and hides behind sofa)

Parent: Ryan, this isn't funny. It's getting late. Come here.

Ryan: (Doesn't hear a word; sits down to do a puzzle)

Parent: Come here! (Gets up and approaches Ryan)

Ryan: (Giggles and runs)

Parent: (Picks up Ryan) Now lie here. Stop squirming! Lie still. Will you stop this! (As parent turns away to pick up a new diaper, a little bare-bottomed toddler is running away.)

I'm sure you've all been there. This tug-of-war can be very tiring for a parent to deal with day after day. I discovered a much better way to gain gleeful cooperation from a young child:

Parent: (Picks up diaper and holds it like a puppet, making it talk in a silly, squeaky voice) Hi, Ryan! I'm Dilly Diaper! Come here and play with me!

Ryan: (Runs over to diaper puppet) Hi, Dilly!

Parent as Diaper: You're such a nice boy. Will you give me a kiss?

Ryan: Yes. (Gives diaper a kiss)

Parent as Diaper: How about a nice hug?

Ryan: (Giggles and hugs diaper)

Parent as Diaper: Lie right here next to me. Right here. Yes. Can I go on you? Oh, yes?! Goody, goody, goody! (The diaper chats with Ryan while he's being changed.)

Parent as Diaper: Oh, Ryan! Listen, I hear your shoes calling you—Ryan! Ryan!

The most amazing thing about this approach is that it works over and over and over. You'll keep thinking, *He's not honestly going to fall for this again, is he?* But he will! Probably the nicest by-products of this method are that you are in a good mood and you have a little fun time with your child.

Mother-Speak

"We were on vacation and our son, Daniel, was getting into trouble and not listening. I had brought along your notes and read through them to see if I could find a tool to help with him. When I came across the talking diaper section of the book, I thought, *No way!* But I decided to try anyway. I used my hand as a puppet. Well, sir, you could have knocked me over with a feather! Not only did he listen, but he absolutely and completely believed my hand was another person! I now also use it with my daughter, and she's just mesmerized by 'Mr. Hand.' She'll ask for him specifically and always listens to what *he* asks her to do. I have told all my friends about it, but I think some of them feel too silly to try it. Me? I say, whatever works, and THIS one definitely works!"

—Ezia, mother to Daniel, age 4, and Sedona, age 2

When you've got a toddler or preschooler, this technique can be a pure lifesaver. I remember one day when my son was almost three. We were waiting in a long line at the grocery store and he was getting antsy. I started making my hand talk to him. It was asking him questions about the items in the cart. Suddenly, he hugged my hand, looked up at me, and said, "Mommy, I love for you to pretend this hand is talking."

It's delightful to see how a potentially negative situation can be turned into a fun experience by changing a child's focus to fun and fantasy. This is a particularly popular parenting skill because once mastered it can be used in virtually any situation to bring pleasant results.

> **Mother-Speak**
>
> "We love doing the cooperation games, making things talk, and making cooperation fun. If life can't be fun for a child, then what's the point in being a child? The adult world is so very serious, there's plenty of time for that. So, with our daughter we try not to take too many things too seriously."
>
> **—Kristi, mother to Arianna, age 3**

Engage the Imagination

A variation on the Make It Talk technique that also works very well is to capitalize on a young child's vivid imagination as a way to thwart negative emotions. You might pretend to find a trail of caterpillars on the way to the store, hop to the car like a kangaroo, or pretend a carrot turns you orange as you eat it. Vegetable soup can be transformed into a magic power brew, a toothbrush can have a voice and locate every speck of food on the teeth as it does its work, or the toys can come alive and make a parade into the toy box.

Children love to pretend, and, by entering their world and playing along with them, you can prevent many skirmishes over everyday chores. Once you open your mind to the possibilities, you'll see that almost any event can be sweetened with a little fun imagination.

Sing a Song

Even if you can't carry a tune, putting anything to music makes you easier to listen to and more fun, too. You can wash your child's hands while singing "This is the way we wash our hands, wash our hands." One mom of five discovered a great way to keep her children content during car rides. She loved to sing, so she made up opera tunes about the scenes she saw as she drove along the road. Her children would often chime in with their own versions.

You can sing whenever the spirit moves you. You can sing songs that you know just to liven up the moment, or you can create a particular song to be used as a cue to certain tasks—such as a cleanup song that takes place whenever the toys are picked up and put away.

A beautiful side effect of putting your words to music is that both you and your child will end up feeling much happier.

Mother-Speak

"I learned the hard way about being too serious versus making a game out of things. One day, Maya and I were going for a walk to the park. When we walked through a neighbor's yard she picked up some pebbles and threw them. I told her that we don't throw rocks. Then I said, 'If you throw those again, then we are going home and not to the park.' She did throw them again, so I picked her up and we started back home. She screamed bloody murder the whole way. I was sure the neighbors were all watching me do the walk of shame home with a screaming child. Long story short, I guess it was good that I kept my word but I learned that lots of times I was going much too quickly to the consequence, without attempting a more pleasant approach first. Now when something like that happens, I am more creative. We usually end up following imaginary caterpillars or marching in a parade to the park. And it's so much nicer for both of us."

—Michelle, mother to Maya, age 3

Tell a Story

Children love stories. These will hold their attention and can get them to willingly do what you want them to do. Stories can be used to teach a lesson, ward off boredom, or keep a child focused on the task at hand.

Stories can be told in advance of any event to let your child know what's about to happen and prevent fussing when the actual event occurs. You can tell a little tale about a boy who goes to Grandma's house for dinner and how he says "please" and "thank you." The grandparents are so proud of him. This is in preparation for an actual visit, of course!

You can tell a story about a puppy who goes to the doctor for a checkup, a dinosaur who visits the dentist, or a penguin's first day at day care. You can use the story format to teach important lessons about sharing, being kind, being patient, or any other life skill you are trying to teach your child.

Mother-Speak

"The storytelling tip is effective with Oscar. He is fascinated with other kids' misbehavior. When he observes a situation he later says, 'You talk about it.' This means he wants me to tell a story about the little boy who wouldn't take turns on the slide or the girl who was yelling at her mommy in the locker room at the Y. Oscar asks me to tell these stories over and over. I think it is very interesting that he's not at all interested in stories about kids who behave well! But I feel he learns from other children's mistakes. Now, Oscar will often tell his dad these stories at the end of the day."

—Nicole, mother to Oscar, age 3

Stories can also be used to keep your child still and mentally occupied, perhaps when you are dressing him, waiting in a long line at the post office, or putting him to bed at night. A storytelling routine can be a handy tool in all of these cases. If you have a talkative, imaginative child, invite him to tell his own stories, too!

Be Silly

Experts say that children laugh about three hundred times a day, but we serious adults laugh less than fifteen times a day, and for many stressed-out parents it's probably much less than that. Not only does laughter reduce stress, lower blood pressure, and boost your immune system, it makes you feel happy, encourages your child to cooperate with you, and ends fussy moods.

Children don't require a scripted comedy show for entertainment. Any lighthearted banter will do the job. Humor—pretending to fall, exaggerated speech, or funny accents—can often create a joyful moment. Being silly—like putting your child's sock on his hand instead of his foot—often elicits a laugh, along with the desired cooperation.

Mother-Speak

"When my children start to whine I say, 'Uh oh, where did your big-boy (big-girl) voice go? Do you know? Is it under the table? In your shoe? Is it in your hair?' Usually one or two questions and they will find their voice in the middle of their shirt and tell me, 'It's right here!' I tell them they better hurry and grab it so it won't get away."

—Marisa, mother to Elijah, age 4, and Marin, age 2

The added benefit to acting silly, just like the other cooperation games, is that it will lighten your spirits as well as your child's. And you may find yourself smiling and laughing a lot more often.

5-3-1 Go! Fair Warning Prevents Battles

When children are immersed in play, they usually put their entire beings into the activity. It is this intensity that allows them to absorb so much about the world in the early years of their life. They are always learning, always taking in something new. Because of this intensity, it can be very hard for a child to switch from one activity to another without first making a mental adjustment.

When a child is in the middle of a wonderful puzzle and a parent calls him to dinner, it's an unusual child who can immediately drop the piece in process and run to the table. (Actually, it's also a rare adult who can leave an activity that quickly.)

You can help your children change activities by giving them time to process the change mentally before they follow through physically. Prior to expecting action from your children, call out a five-minute alert, then a three-minute alert, and, finally, a one-minute alert. Watch how this happens:

Julie and Alex are happily playing at the park while Mom is reading on a bench nearby. She gets up, comes over to them, and at eye level announces, "We are going to leave the park in five minutes." (She holds up five fingers.) She returns to her bench to read. A few minutes later, she calls out, "Julie! Alex! We are leaving in three minutes!" (Holds up three fingers.) A few minutes later: "One minute." (One finger is raised.) A minute later, "Do you want to have one more slide or one more swing before we go?" After the final slide, Mom announces that it's time to leave. Her children don't respond immediately, so she segues into a fun choice to get things moving: "Do you want to run to the car or hop like bunnies?" Almost immediately the two kids begin to hop toward the car.

This type of counting is different from the typical countdown to disaster, "1 . . . 2 . . . 3. Okay, now you're in trouble! Time-out!" The 5-3-1 Go! method is a respectful way of letting your child know in advance what's coming up and allowing her to finish what she's into so that she can make the transition. Use 5-3-1 Go! daily as a way to help your child cooperate with you on many tasks, such as getting dressed, finishing lunch, putting away toys, getting into the bathtub, getting out of the bathtub, and getting ready for bed.

Mother-Speak

"I've been using 5-3-1 Go! with Anna and it works like a charm. The biggest challenge was training my adult friends that when I started the countdown, it meant them, too! Sometimes I'd get to 'Go' and my friends would want to continue to chat. Now my friends know that when I start the countdown, I mean it for us as well as the children."

—Tracy, mother to Anna, age 4, and Zack, age 2

Eye-to-Eye Discussions

Very often parents call out instructions to their children from two rooms away. The children are engaged in their play and barely hear the instructions, let alone understand it's directed at them. Or, parents talk "at" their children, lecturing in a monologue that invites no true communication. Children of all ages respond much better to purposeful, face-to-face conversation.

You can engage your child's attention much more effectively if you take a moment to go to her, get down to her eye level, and talk to her face-to-face. When you do this, you have your child's full attention. There's no chance that you're being ignored or that she doesn't realize you are talking to her. In addition, your child can read your nonverbal communication signs, such as facial expression and body language. This will add to her ability to truly understand what you are saying. At the same time, you will be able to read your child's nonverbal language, which will help you know if she truly understands what you are saying.

Children are not little adults, but they are little people. They love their parents and they want to understand them. Give them an opportunity to listen, learn, and participate in a conversational exchange with you.

When you have a request, or have something to say, take the extra minute or two to get to eye level with your child and talk to her—clearly and respectfully. Explain what you want and why you want it. Ask questions to confirm that your child understands you. This exchange of information doesn't take very long, and the pleasant results are well worth it.

Mother-Speak

"It is a useful reminder that children need more explanation. We adults take so many things for granted and can sometimes unwittingly forget that our children don't have our lifetime of experience behind them. We unconsciously expect our children to know more than they do when it comes to their behavior."

—**Sonja, mother to Ekatarina, age 3,**
and Aleksandar, age 1

Use Positive Words

Some of the most overused words in parenting are *no*, *don't*, and *stop*. It is necessary, of course, that we get our children to stop misbehaviors. However, when these words are overused, they create more problems than they solve. I call these *fighting words* because when you start your sentence with any of these words your child doesn't even hear or comprehend what comes next, and the "fighting word" acts as a fuse to set off a tantrum.

When possible, make an attempt to phrase your words in the positive, rather than the negative.

Negative Fighting Words	Positive Cooperation Words
Stop fighting over that truck!	Please share the truck nicely.
Don't hit the baby!	Touch the baby gently.
No, you can't have ice cream.	You can have a banana or a piece of cheese right now.

When this optimistic approach to language choices becomes more common in your home, you will find your children imitating this style of speaking, so it's not just a cooperation tool, it's training for a lifetime of positive communication skills.

When/Then, Now/Later, You May/After You

Often, when parents don't want children to do something it's not the act that's the problem for the parent, it's the timing. Candy before dinner is a no-go but after dinner is fine. Playing outside after dark isn't allowed, but playing outside after lunch is great. The When/Then technique teaches children the proper timing and sequence of events. It is a wonderful approach because it respects and acknowledges your child's desires but moves your child's action to the correct place in time.

Another lovely benefit to this method is that it is a great way to avoid saying those fighting words (*no*, *don't*, *stop*) quite so many times in a day. Here are a few examples:

- **When** you put your pajamas on, **then** we can read a story.
- Eat your lunch **now**, and then you can have a piece of candy **later** when you finish lunch.
- **You may** play outside **after you** clean up your toys.

You'll notice that this pattern has a very pleasant feel to it. You are telling your child that, yes, he can do the thing he wants to do, but after he does the thing you request of him. Or, to put it another way, yes, he can do what he wants, but later.

Mother-Speak

"The wonderful thing about the When/Then technique is that you are, in effect, giving your children the power to make something happen. They feel in control, and they learn that they can be responsible people who make good decisions. You accomplish your goal of getting them to cooperate with you . . . and everyone's happy!"

—Barb, mother to Caroline, age 4, and George, age 3

Distraction and Redirection

Distraction can be a lifesaver when an insignificant issue is at hand and you're just too tired to be otherwise creative or it's just such a minor issue that it's not worth getting into it. It can also work to end fussiness and tantrums before they really get rolling. A child who is in the middle of a low-level fuss can often be

Yasmin, age 18 months

distracted by the mention of a cat walking on the front lawn or a butterfly flitting by. Or, he can be given a pepper shaker with a white napkin to sprinkle the pepper on or another interesting task to carry out.

Distractions can be part of a usual routine in some cases. Some examples are a flashlight used during diaper-changing, a shoe box of special toys to be used when Mommy or Daddy is on the telephone, or a child's backpack filled with fun activities to take along on car, bus, or airplane rides.

Redirection is when you purposely alter a child's attention from one thing to another. For example, if your child is getting frustrated while putting together a puzzle and you sense a tantrum is building up, it's sometimes best to move him away from the puzzle and direct his attention to a different play activity. If two siblings

Mothers-Speak

"Here's an idea that works well for us: I send the children outside to play and let them run. Fresh air and exercise can help everyone feel happier."

—**Suzanne, mother to Laetitia, age 4, and Clément, age 10 months**

"After a particularly trying day, I 'transferred' my daughter and myself onto my bike for a lovely long ride. We both rode silently enjoying nature and the wind in our hair. Our moods calmed, and we shared smiles when we returned for a quick dip in the pool and then a nursing session. In unison, we forgot our troubles and reconnected."

—**Lynne, mother to Erika, age 2, and Colin, age 6**

are getting on each other's nerves, you might send one off to a different room to run an errand for you. If your child is getting bored and whiny, bundle him up and take him for a walk.

Distraction and redirection are particularly helpful for families who have more than one young child in the household. If you have to deal with every single fuss, whine, and struggle, you will make yourself a bit crazy. Instead, be willing to fall back on the distraction technique from time to time to keep your sanity and maintain peace in the house.

Family Rules: A Key to Peace

Even the youngest child can grasp the idea of a rule. It may be a simple daily ritual, such as "We brush our teeth before bed" or "We take our plates to the sink after we eat." Or it can be a guide to behavior, such as "We don't hit." Rules work best if they are short, simply stated, and consistently followed.

The first thing you need to do is to decide on your top rules. Too many rules make life complicated. And, when there are too many rules they are easily forgotten, so you'll want to determine your top ten or so. The best way to figure out your top ten is to make a list of the behavior issues that most bother you. When you see what these are, you'll know which issues are most important to address with a formal rule.

Once you've made a list of your top behavior issues, translate each one into a clear, simple rule. For example, if your children are too rough with each other and often push, hit, kick, pull hair, or wrestle to the point of tears, then come up with a simple easy-to-understand rule that will encompass all such behaviors, such as "No hurting each other."

As you create your rules, make sure they are ones you can and will enforce. This isn't a wish list of every nice thing you hope for;

Mother-Speak

"When I was in college studying to be a teacher, I took a class on behavior management that covered rule making. The professor recommended making the rules a positive experience from the beginning. Instead of creating the rules yourself, have the children make them up with you. You could shout, 'Is this how we should talk in the house?' Children: 'No, we should use our quiet voices.' Adult: 'So, what should that rule say?' Children: 'No yelling.' Having them involved in this way makes them feel that they are a part of making the rules and more inclined to follow them."

—Genevieve, mother to Matthew, age 2

it's the top behaviors that you expect and are willing to enforce consistently.

A great way to proclaim the new rules is to make a family rules poster. Use bright colors and decorations to make it friendlier, and then place it on the wall for all to see and remember.

Another advantage to specific, written rules is that they carry with them additional implied rules. "No hurting each other" may have been created to curb the physical fighting between your children, but it also implies no emotional hurting. Rules reflect a family's personality and culture—the values and morals that guide all of your actions and establish what's most important in your family unit.

Mother-Speak

"I always know when Eva is hungry because she starts whining, fussing, and badgering me for cookies [*solve the real problem*]. If I say no for any reason, a meltdown ensues [*avoid fighting words*]. Lately I've discovered that kneeling down and asking her if she's hungry [*eye to eye*] and offering her a selection of some healthy snacks [*choices*] tends to defuse her. I tell her when she calms down, then she can pick her snack [*When/Then technique*]. I finish by taking her to the cabinet to get her selection [*distraction*]."

—**Jocelyn, mother to Elena, age 5; Eva, age 3; and Rory, age 18 months**

Make It Brief, Make It Clear

In an effort to be a good parent, many people say way too much, turning an intended lesson into a lecture of wasted words and negative energy. Children often tune out after the first few sentences. (You can usually tell by that glazed look in their eyes!) And while you may be trying hard to teach an important lesson, if you carry on with a long and involved dissertation, your child may not understand a single word.

The less you say, the more your child will hear, understand, and remember. So get your child's eye-to-eye attention and then make a short, concise statement. Repeat yourself if necessary, but don't elaborate and lecture.

Think It, Say It, Mean It, Do It

A common complaint from parents is that their child "doesn't ever listen to me" or "won't do what I ask the first time." As frustrating as this is, I must inform you that the main reason children don't listen to their parents is because their parents don't require it. This is a common mistake that even the best parents make. They repeat a request over and over and over, until they either explode or give up. To compound the problem, the first request made is not well planned, so it isn't followed through to the end.

For example, a parent calls to a child that it's time to leave the house but then gets busy with something along the way. A bit later, the parent calls, "Ready to go!" but again gets sidetracked on the way to the door. Only after a few more rounds of this game is the parent actually—finally—ready to leave. The child, in the meantime, has been ignoring all requests made. Another example is a parent who asks a child to clean up his toys. After several more requests, the parent realizes how late it is and rounds the child up for bed (cleaning up the toys after said child is asleep). For a slightly older child, a parent likely adds a monologue about "why do I have to always clean up myself?"

If done once, this *asking, not meaning it, and not following through* wouldn't be a big problem, but since the pattern happens frequently, the child learns that the parent's requests are optional.

It can significantly simplify your life if you will adhere to this blueprint as often as possible:

- Think through your needs first.
- Make a clear and specific request.
- Follow through (with calm and purpose) if your child doesn't comply.

Daily Routines: Predictability Triumphs

Children respond to predictable patterns in their lives. These routines function as subconscious cues as to how they should act or what they should do. Very often, though, the routines that they are following have happened accidentally and are contrary to what parents really want. For instance, a child may have a routine of falling asleep on the sofa to the sound of the television. The parents bemoan the fact that he won't fall asleep in bed, but since he falls asleep on the sofa night after night, it is his routine.

Consistency and routine create feelings of security and reliability in your child's life. It's a very big world, and children learn so much every day that they can easily become overwhelmed with the enormity of it all. When certain important key points are always the same, these things create anchors of security. Young children look for these anchors and thrive on their consistency. They enjoy routines and easily adapt to them, even looking for them. So it is far better if we *create* the routines we want them to follow. If we don't create routines, children will adopt their own, similar to the little boy who sleeps on the sofa.

If we aren't happy with the way our days are flowing now, we can change our child's current routines to ones that we choose. Children adapt easily, and when something happens consistently in their lives, they will look for it to continue in that same way.

I remember one Sunday morning a long time ago when my husband woke early to discover our boys, David and Coleton, already

Matthew Jr., age 2

awake. Since they were the only ones awake in the house, Daddy decided to take them out to breakfast. The following Sunday morning our girls were away at sleepovers, and I was busy writing, so Daddy decided to again take the boys out for breakfast. The third week, Robert and I were awakened by the boys standing at the side of our bed. "Daddy! Wake up!" they were whispering. "It's Sunday and we *always* go out to breakfast on Sunday!"

In my sons' analysis of their world, two weeks in a row equaled "always," creating a new routine for them. If you think about this, it may bring to mind similar situations that have occurred with your child—a certain book that *must* be read, a specific path your stroll *must* follow, a certain order a game *must* take, a particular phrase that *must* be said before you leave the house or turn out the lights for sleep.

We can take advantage of this natural desire children have for routine by creating specific routines to help the days flow more smoothly. Since most children share the same reasoning as my sons about "always," it takes thirty days or less for them to adopt a new routine as normal.

It can be helpful to think about the key points in your days and jot down how these actions will fit together. For example, does it bother you when your children run around in their pajamas all morning? Do you prefer that your children get dressed before breakfast? Then make that part of your daily routine. Do you hate waking up to a family room cluttered with toys? Make toy cleanup part of the pre-bedtime routine. Once your children fall into the familiar pattern of action, it will happen without stress or nagging, making your home happier and more peaceful for all.

To create your daily routine, write down the approximate times and sequence of key family events, such as waking, dressing, eat-

Parent-Speak

"We both work full-time, and we have a nanny care for our twins while we're at work. She has them on a great schedule. For a while we both ignored that schedule on the weekends because we just wanted to relax and play with them. However, we saw the behavior differences were extreme. They were calm and happy during the week, but they were cranky and needy and had more tantrums on the weekends. Once we realized this, we began to keep them on the weekday schedule for the weekends, too. We really see the difference when they wake, eat, and sleep on schedule versus when they don't. It has really helped keep the crankiness and tantrums to a minimum."

—Lorraine and Alan, parents to Marc and Mira, age 2

ing, playtime, cleanup time, nap time, and bedtime. Decide how you'd like your days to proceed. Fashion a poster listing the main events. To take this one step further, you can also create your family rules as described earlier and add them to the poster. Now you have a daily guideline to follow.

Keep in mind that no routine is made to be set in stone. No rules are absolute. You can be flexible when you decide to. However, purposefully *choosing* to veer off your routine or rules is far different than accidentally falling into chaos!

Just a note here for those of you who *don't* live by routines and those who *don't* like to follow or create routines. As in all parenting advice, the overriding tenet is to do what works for you. If your family functions beautifully in a relaxed go-with-the-flow sort of way, then don't change a thing. Any new idea is only worth exploring if you think it will make your life easier or happier.

Success with Happy Face Cards

Many children respond well to a visual reminder about how to behave appropriately. A Happy Face poster is a wonderful method of allowing children to understand the impact of their behavior choices. Here's how it works:

1. Make a list of your top three to five rules. Make them easy to understand. Print them clearly in large letters. (Examples: No hurting people. Do what Mommy or Daddy tells you to do. No tantrums. No screaming.) Hang the list on the wall, at your child's eye level and in a location near where your child spends most of the day.

2. Use oversized index cards or cut a piece of poster board into ten squares, about 3″ × 5″. On the front side of ten pieces draw a colorful happy face, or find happy faces online and

print and paste them onto the squares. Your child can even help decorate the happy faces, if you'd like. On the back side of each card, draw a blue sad face. You'll start with ten happy/sad face squares. After a week or two, if desired, you can reduce this number to eight and then eventually five.

3. Hang the faces—happy side up—near the rules. Tell your child that every morning they will all be happy faces. Each time he breaks a rule, one face will change to sad.
4. Each day after dinner count the faces with your child.

Some children respond well to this approach without any attached rewards or consequences. Just seeing the sad face is enough to help them identify and curb bad behaviors. Other children need or like to have a small reward connected. You can include a reward system, based on the number of happy faces remaining at the end of each day. For example, your child gets to pick the same number of books as happy faces for prebedtime reading, or he gets to choose a game to play with you for that number of minutes. Or, perhaps he gets the same number of small marshmallows for a treat after dinner. Therefore, five happy faces equals five books, five minutes of his game, or five marshmallows. This gives your child a concrete way to understand that his choices and his behavior affect outcomes in his life.

Just a note here: when you change a happy face to a sad one your child may have a meltdown! He may even rip it off the wall. If he does, you must VERY CALMLY say, "I'm sorry this happened, but because you [insert behavior] there is now a sad face." Unwrinkle the sad face and tape it back up. If your child displays great unhappiness when you turn a face over, you will know that the system is working as it should! You *want* your child to be unhappy about his misbehavior and the consequences it brings. This leads to better self-discipline and will help him to make decisions about how to act.

Explain the happy face idea to your child completely when you begin. Your conversation might sound something like this:

> Honey, I want you to know that I love you and you are very important to me. As a mommy, it is my job to make sure that you grow up to be a nice person. Some things have been happening that make me sad, like when you don't listen to me, or when you hit your sister, or when you yell and stomp your feet. We are going to do something to help you stop making these mistakes. I am going to put two things on the wall. This is the first thing. It is our rules. Let's read it. [Read and discuss the rules.] This is the second thing. These are your happy face cards. Happy faces mean you are doing the right things. A sad face tells you that you did the wrong thing. You want to try not to have sad faces. After dinner every day we will count the happy faces. You will get to pick out that many books to read with Mommy and that many marshmallows to eat after dinner. Do you understand how the happy faces work?

Once you've established this program, stick with it every single day for about a month. Monitor the changes in your child's behavior. If all is going well, continue as you are until you feel that good behaviors are set in place. At that time, take down the poster and see how things progress. If your child's behavior backslides, reestablish the program.

Time-Out: Why, When, and How

Time-out is a traditional and often-used discipline technique. But time-out is not a magical answer to all discipline problems, and, if overused, it can lose its effectiveness. However, it can be a valuable, positive parenting tool when used selectively and in conjunction with all of the other skills discussed in this book.

A time-out works because it interrupts a child's negative behavior, separates him from the problem or situation that is igniting his emotions, and allows him to calm himself down. Putting a child in

Key Point

A time-out is not meant to be a punishment. It is a method to stop a specific misbehavior and help a child learn how to calm himself and control his behavior.

- A time-out itself stops misbehavior but doesn't necessarily correct it. The critical final step should occur once parent and child are calm. This is when the teaching should take place.

- Let the child know—briefly, concisely, and politely—why he was in a time-out and how he can avoid going there again. Teach, don't scold or lecture, and try to keep it brief. After you have explained why what he did was wrong, ask him to apologize for his misbehavior.

- You don't have to hold a grudge or stay angry at your child to make a point; the time-out has achieved the purpose of identifying that his behavior was wrong. At this teaching step, you don't have to hold back a hug or an "I love you." This is the time to show your child that he can make mistakes, and he can learn from them. And maybe most important, that he can be in the wrong and be forgiven, respected, and loved.

a time-out has a purpose for a parent, too—it allows you to separate from a youngster whose behavior is upsetting you, allowing you to calm down as well.

Keep the following tips in mind when using time-outs for your child:

- Decide on which issues will warrant a time-out and make them clear to your child. Issues such as backtalk, hitting, or destructiveness are perfectly suited to this method. As much as a time-out may seem to be a good solution for tantrums, that sometimes isn't the case. You'll have to drag a kicking, flailing child to the time-out spot, and he'll often get right back up again.

• Use a safe, boring location for time-outs to occur. A child-proofed bathroom, laundry room, and hallway are all good choices. Young or sensitive children can find banished isolation frightening or disturbing, so it can escalate the problem. In that case, consider using a chair, step, or vacant corner in the same room where you are for the time-out. Avoid using a child's bedroom, playroom, or favorite chair for this purpose, as you don't want to create a negative experience in a play or sleeping space.

• There are two ways to decide how long to keep a child in a time-out. The common rule of thumb is one minute per year of age, which matches well with a child's age-related maturity. The second option is to keep him there until he is calmed down, which could be less or more than the minute method.

• If your child refuses to stay in a time-out, do *not* fight with him, sit on him, or lock him in a room. Depending on your child's personality, and yours, use one of these ideas:

  • Make sure that you've explained a time-out and that your child is old enough to understand what it means.

  • Practice time-out when your child is *not* misbehaving so he'll know what you expect when it does occur. You can even role-play and pretend to be your child. Show exactly what you expect him to do during a time-out.

  • When you use a time-out, walk your child to the time-out spot. Calmly instruct him to sit. If he pops up, say, "No, sit." Gently guide him to sit back down. Repeat as many times as necessary.

  • Sit *with* your child in a small room. Don't talk or lecture. Just sit.

  • Have the time-out occur wherever your child happens to be. Stand above him, cross your arms, maintain a stern face, and announce, "You are in a time-out."

- If your child has stopped the misbehavior, then consider the time-out over—even if it lasted only ten seconds. (After all, that's the purpose of a time-out—to stop the misbehavior.)

- If your child cries, yells, or stomps while in a time-out—let him. He is upset and he should be. Don't allow swearing or destructive behavior, but do allow him to be mad.

- If your child comes out of the time-out and repeats the behavior that sent him there in the first place—return him to a time-out. And again. And again. This is perfectly normal, as children often need repeat lessons to learn. If you are consistent, he will eventually learn the behavior is unacceptable and you mean what you say.

- If a time-out doesn't work for your child, it's possible that it's been used too many times, for too many reasons, or in a way that doesn't clearly convey its purpose. Either revise how you use it or discard this technique and use other discipline tools instead.

It's Okay to Have Fun, It's Okay to Be Firm

You don't *always* have to use a clever skill to get your child to cooperate with you. There are plenty of times when you'll just want to say it straight up. When you do, try to follow these basic rules:

- **Get eye to eye.** Remember there is no calling from a distance, no mumbled directions.
- **Say what you mean.** Don't make threats; don't use empty words.
- **Be clear and specific.** Don't make vague requests; don't make your child guess what you want.
- **Be polite.** "Please" and "thank you" are magic words for parents to use, too.
- **Stay calm.** Anger just makes things worse.

- **Follow through with action.** Take him by the hand; put on his shoes; put away the toy. *Help* your child do what you asked him to do.
- **Be consistent.** The more you follow these steps the easier it gets for both of you.

Be Flexible, Don't Fret, and Pick Your Battles

Often a person's desire to be a great parent puts too much stress on everyone in the household because it's an impossible goal. In life, most things don't fall in the critical category and can be handled in many different ways with fine results. You don't have to be a perfect parent to raise wonderful children.

Daddy; Nathan, age 1; and Mommy

Father-Speak

"I have been getting really stressed out with my children lately. I finally realized that I was overmanaging every single behavior of each child. No matter what they said or did, I had to show them a better way. When I decided to back off a bit and address only the important issues, there were no resulting disasters and we all became much more relaxed."

—**Matthew, father to Megan, age 7; Jack, age 5; and Evan, age 2**

Remove the emotion and analysis that clutters up your head and try to see daily situations for what they really are. Then look for a solution. A spilled glass of milk isn't a sign your child is clumsy, careless, or irresponsible; it's just a spill. It calls for a sponge. A toddler's wet pants do not mean he'll be in diapers until first grade. Nor are they an indication that you've totally failed Potty Training 101. They aren't even an act of willful disobedience on his part. They are just a product of a busy child who didn't make it to the bathroom on time and who needs a change. Two siblings bickering over a toy doesn't mean they hate each other, it doesn't mean your children are selfish or greedy, nor does it mean you've failed your job as a parent. It just means that they both want the same toy and don't know how to settle their dispute.

Pick your battles. Not every issue needs to be addressed and corrected. Little things can sometimes slip through the cracks with no impact on anything of importance. As a matter of fact, if you feel you must address every single episode of misbehavior of any size, you will likely drive yourself and your children crazy! Every once in awhile, the best thing you can do for family peace is to turn around, pretend you didn't see it, take a deep breath, and move on to something else.

> **Key Point**
> "Kind words can be short and easy to speak, but their echoes are truly endless."
>
> **—Mother Teresa**

Most of today's biggest parenting issues can be solved in many different ways. No matter the approach, they are soon resolved and new ones will take their place. If during the course of your days you can remember to use your parenting techniques, to try to be flexible and relaxed, and to pick your battles wisely, you'll find your child more willing to cooperate in most issues. At the same time, you keep calm, peaceful, and in control. And best of all, you'll enjoy raising your child much, much more.

Compliments, Encouragement, and Kind Words

Children—just like all human beings—respond well to positive words. A child's world is full of negative input, orders, corrections, and criticism. When children receive compliments, encouragement, and kind words, it helps them feel great about themselves and their world. It builds their self-esteem. It encourages more of the behavior that prompted the positive feedback.

As parents we sometimes take our roles so seriously that we try too hard to be the ever-present teacher. We want our children to grow up right, so we take every opportunity to correct their path. We need to understand that our kind words can sometimes teach as much—or more—than our corrections can. No child has been harmed by too much encouragement or by thinking that her parent loves her a little bit too much, so relax and *say* all those positive thoughts that are rolling around in your head.

During their growth and development, children go through many stages of self-doubt. They compare themselves to others, or to our expectations for them, and they often see themselves as coming up short. As parents, we can offset this natural tendency in our children by providing them with plenty of encouraging support, which will endow them with the skills to think more positively, which in turn will help them make better choices about their behavior. Children take many cues about who they are from their interactions with their parents. We want to help them paint a picture of themselves as responsible, capable human beings who make good choices and behave appropriately.

> **Key Point**
> "I don't believe that children can develop in a healthy way unless they feel that they have value apart from anything they own or any skill that they learn. They need to feel they enhance the life of someone else, that they are needed. Who, better than parents, can let them know that?"
> —**Fred Rogers, "Mister Rogers' Neighborhood"**

Build a Foundation of Love, Trust, and Respect

In their efforts to be good teachers, many parents treat their children in ways that they would never treat a friend. In their efforts to raise respectable children, they become so focused on the end goal

Amelia, age 3½

that they don't realize that the primary message coming through to their children is not a pleasant one.

Imagine that you've been invited to a friend's home for dinner. Your friend welcomes you at the door and you step inside. Suddenly, your host shouts, "What is the matter with you! Your shoes are all muddy and you're getting my carpet dirty!" Embarrassed, you mumble, "Sorry" and remove your shoes. As you do, you notice the hole in your sock, and so does your friend, who announces, "Geez. Don't you think you could have dressed properly for dinner? You look like a slob." As you take your place at the table, your host knocks your elbow off the table with a whispered, "Tsk, tsk. Where are your manners?" The dinner conversation is primarily your friend's story about a guest who joined them for dinner last night who had *lovely* manners and no holes in her socks. The story is sprinkled with your friend's occasional admonishments about your table manners. When you finish your meal, you stand up only to hear your friend say, "It sure would be nice if *somebody* helped clear the table."

Take a close look at your own daily interactions with your children. Check to be sure that you aren't so focused on improving your child's behavior that your approach is too insensitive or unforgiving. Make sure that the primary message to your child is *I love you, I believe in you, and I respect you.* Children who are confident that they are loved and respected by the important adults in their lives will respond overall in a much more pleasant way.

How do you get this message through to your children? **First,** by giving them what they want most from you—your time. **Second,** give them your ear. Children thrive when they have someone who really listens to them. Sometimes it's not as important to give advice and solve problems as it is to just plain listen. **Third,** praise and encourage your children daily. Look for reasons, big and small, to give your children positive feedback. **Fourth,** tell them you love them. Tell them you believe in them. Tell them you respect them. Use your words and your actions to convey *I love you, I believe in you, and I respect you.*

Reminder Page
No-Cry Discipline Parenting Skills and Tools

- First: Solve the real problem: Tired? Hungry? Frustrated? Bored? Overstimulated? Scared? Confused?
- Be consistent.
- Offer a choice.
- Play a cooperation game.
- Make it talk.
- Engage the imagination.
- Sing a song.
- Tell a story.
- Be silly.
- Use 5-3-1 Go! (Give fair warning.)
- Have an eye-to-eye discussion.
- Use positive words. (Avoid *no, don't, stop*.)
- Use when/then, now/later, you may/after you.
- Distract and redirect.
- Use family rules.
- Make it brief, make it clear.
- Think it, say it, mean it, do it.
- Follow daily routines.
- Use happy face cards.
- Use a time-out to interrupt misbehavior and calm emotions.
- Be firm—it's okay.
- Be flexible. Don't fret. Pick your battles.
- Give compliments, encouragement, and kind words.
- Build a foundation of love, trust, and respect.

Tantrums, Fussing, and Whining

The Big Three

Tantrum—an uncontrolled display of negative emotion or bad temper

Fussing—excessive and unwarranted crying, complaining, and protesting

Whining—carrying on in a mournful, high-pitched (extremely annoying) voice

If you asked people to list the most frustrating, ongoing discipline problems during the early childhood years, you would probably find that these three items appear on almost every parent's and caregiver's list. Some children start these behaviors at two years old (those notorious terrible twos), and some wait until they are closer to age four. Some children are champion whiners but rarely fuss or tantrum, and some are grand tantrumers, rarely whining or fussing. Some children put most of their energy into fussing and just dabble in whining and tantrums. Yet every child masters his or her own adaptation of these three behaviors, which means every parent has to deal with them—no one is exempt!

Controlling Their Emotions

Most often, whining, fussing, and tantrums are caused by a child's inability to express or control his emotions, and this is further complicated by the influence of other people's demands and external conditions. Tiredness, hunger, frustration, and many of the other causes that ignite "the big three" can frequently be avoided, modified, or eliminated. When you can pinpoint the root reason for your child's unpleasant behavior and address that issue directly, you can calm your child and stop the whining or tantrum in its tracks. If you become very observant and learn how to identify your child's emotional triggers *before* they can be set off, you may be able to prevent many negative situations from even happening.

When your child begins a meltdown, stop, look, and think to determine if you can tell what underlying issue is causing the problem. Most children have meltdowns because of the same repeated reasons. Once you understand what these reasons are, you will be able to make changes to reduce the tantrums, fussing, and whining that occur. The following chart includes a list of many likely reasons and some possible solutions.

Reason for Tantrums, Fussing, or Whining	Possible Solutions
Overtiredness	• Provide a quiet, relaxing activity (reading, puzzle, movie). • Put child down for a rest or a nap or put to bed. • Revise the daily nap time/bedtime schedule. • Solve night-waking or other sleep disturbances.
Hunger or Thirst	• Give child a nutritious, nonsugary snack. • Provide something to drink (milk, low-sugar juice, or water). • Revise daily meal and snack schedule.

Reason for Tantrums, Fussing, or Whining	Possible Solutions
Frustration	• Help child achieve his or her goal (e.g., assist with the puzzle, pour the milk). • Provide supervised practice so your child can master whatever skill is leading to the frustration. • Remove the source of the frustration. • Use distraction (get child involved in something else).
Fear/Anxiety/Embarrassment	• Hug, hold, or cuddle your child. • Remove child from difficult situation. • Help him identify and understand his feelings (explain what's happening). • Teach child ways to cope with his emotions.
Unhappiness After Complying with Your Request	• Let him be unhappy (if, for example, it is because you said no cookie, stop running, or don't jump). • Allow him to express his feelings about not being able to do what he wants to do (as long as he complied with your request).
Inability to Communicate	• Try to figure out what your child wants. • Teach a nonverbal child basic sign language. • Calmly encourage him to tell you or show you. • Help him by getting him started on what to say: "Please say, 'Mommy, I need help.' "

Reason for Tantrums, Fussing, or Whining	Possible Solutions
Resistance to Change (Leaving a Place or an Activity)	• Give child a five-minute, a three-minute, and then a one-minute warning. This allows time for child to make the adjustment from one activity to the next. (See 5-3-1 Go! on page 81.) • Offer a choice. "Do you want to walk to the car or run?" • In the future, verbally rehearse child's schedule in advance of the event (so she knows what to expect).
Overstimulation	• Move child away from the activity to a quiet place (e.g., the bathroom for a visit or the kitchen for a snack). • Get down to your child's level, maintain eye contact, and talk in a soothing tone of voice. • Put your child on your lap and your arms around him for a quiet hug.
Boredom	• Provide a toy to play with. • Initiate a word game or I Spy game for distraction. • Tell a story. • Take child outside to play. • Give your child a small task to do. "Can you find the box of macaroni?" "Can you snap these beans?" "Will you go get my slippers for me?" "Can you pick out a new toy for the baby?"
Discomfort	• Determine the issue and see if it can be solved. (Shoes too tight? Socks too bumpy? Too hot? Too cold? Uncomfortable car seat?)

Reason for Tantrums, Fussing, or Whining	Possible Solutions
Sickness or Pain	• Watch your child's behavior for clues to illness. (Undetected ear infection? Teething? Headache? Tummy ache? Undetected allergies or asthma?)
Confusion	• Decide if you are expecting something different of your child every day when this particular issue is involved. • Create routines for everyday occurrences. • Create and post family rules.
Neediness	• Determine if your child's need is warranted. If it is, stop the child's misbehavior and *then* provide the attention she seeks. (If neediness is a sign of another problem, deal with the root issue: Boredom? Divert child to an activity. Shyness? Slowly introduce child to the new situation. Tiredness? Put her down for a nap or to bed.)

Mother-Speak

"When I got upset at my daughter I found myself telling her, 'Sorry, honey, Mommy is really tired right now and that makes me more frustrated.' Then I thought, *Wow, that's the same reason she gets upset, too.* I think we just forget that our kids really are humans like we are, with needs, desires, and frustrations that affect their behavior."

—Kristi, mother to Arianna, age 3

Tips for Handling Tantrums, Fussing, and Whining

No matter how diligent you are in reading and recognizing your child's needs and emotions, your child will still have meltdown moments—or even meltdown days. The following tips can help you handle these inevitable bumps in the road. Look through and study these tips in advance of the next episode. You might even keep them handy so that in a moment of need you'll have some options to consider. (See Reminder Page: Stop the Tantrums, Fussing, and Whining, on page 125.)

Remember that all children are different, all parents are different, and all situations are different. So the ideas that you use may change from situation to situation, from child to child, and from day to day. Be flexible and practice with those solutions that seem to bring you the best results.

- **Offer choices.** You may be able to avoid problems by giving your child more of a say in her life. You can do this, while still maintaining control, by offering your child choices, as discussed previously. Children who are busy deciding what to do next are often distracted away from their emotional outbursts.
- **Get eye to eye.** Making a casual request from five feet above and twenty feet away will likely result in your child ignoring you. This noncompliance creates stress that often leads to fussing and tantrums—from both of you. Instead, get down to your child's level and look him in the eye and make clear, concise requests. This style of communicating will catch his full attention.
- **Validate her feelings.** When your child is having an emotional time, help her identify and understand her emotions. Give words to her feelings. "You're really sad. You want to stay here and play. I know." Of course this doesn't mean you must give in to her

request, but sometimes just letting her know that you understand her problem is enough to help her calm down.

- **Let it happen naturally.** If your child doesn't calm down with gentle efforts, then sometimes it's best to let the tantrum run its course. Children have strong emotions, and at times they need to release them in their own way. If your child doesn't respond to your help, and as long as her fussing or tantrum is not dangerous to her or to property, feel free to say, "I'm leaving the room. Come and get me when you're done." And do just that. Busy yourself with something else (peeking in on her, of course), and wait patiently for your child to calm down.

- **Create a calm-down room.** If tantrums, fussing, or whining are a daily occurrence, then let your child know in advance that all such behavior will take place in one specific room, such as a spare bedroom, the bathroom, or the laundry room. (Avoid using a child's bedroom or playroom for this.) Once there he can let go of his feelings and come out when he has calmed down—you might call this the calm-down room or the peaceful room.

Put something in the room that can assist your child in calming down. Leave a number of comforting stuffed animals, a pillow, and a blanket in the room. You might provide a CD player with relaxing lullaby music or a white noise machine. These play the sounds of ocean waves or rainfall and are a great help in achieving relaxation. Turn on the music or sounds when your child goes to the room, or, even better, show your child how to work the machine.

Let's say that your child is having frequent daily tantrums. At a time when you are both relaxed, explain that you've created a special room just for him when he is upset and not in control. Explain exactly what a tantrum looks like (give a demonstration). Let your child know that when this happens, he'll need to move to the calm-down room. Show him how to turn on his music or white noise. When a tantrum starts, you can escort your child to the room with one brief comment, "You can come out when you're done." If he comes out of the room and is still having the tantrum, just lead him back, repeating, "You can come out when you're done." You might even choose to stay with him.

When your child calms down and comes out of the room, then it is time to deal with whatever issue upset him—if it still needs to be addressed. If the tantrum occurred over a trivial issue, then it's best to just leave it in the past and move on to the next activity.

At first your child may spend the whole day in the calm-down room, but he will learn how to calm himself and control his emotions—an important life skill.

- **Teach deep breathing and relaxation (the Quiet Bunny).** When children get worked up, their breathing often becomes rapid and shallow and their bodies become rigid. These physiological symptoms can keep a child in an agitated state and prevent relaxation. You can teach your child how to relax her body and then use this approach when whining, fussing, or tantrums begin.

This technique is easier to use in times of stress if your child is familiar and comfortable with it. You may want to end each day or start each morning with a brief relaxation session that you do together. If you practice yoga, you can use some of your familiar moves, or check out one of the many books available about yoga for children.

If you prefer a simpler idea, just coach your child through a brief exercise I call the Quiet Bunny:

> Let's be a Quiet Bunny.
> Close your eyes.
> Relax.
> Breathe in. Breathe out.
> It's time for the bunny to relax.
> Wiggle your bunny nose. Now make your bunny face be still and relax.

Wiggle your toes. Now make your toes relax.
Wiggle your fingers. Now make your fingers relax.
(You can add more body parts, such as arms, shoulders, and
    legs if your child has the patience or need.)
Breathe in. Breathe out.
Relax.
Now you are a quiet bunny.

This can be a very helpful technique with children since they can be susceptible to your gentle suggestions of relaxation. Once your child is familiar with this process, you can call upon it whenever he is agitated (or getting you agitated!). Crouch down to your child's level, put your hands on his shoulders, look him in the eye, and say, "Let's do our Quiet Bunny." Then talk him through the process. Over time, you won't have to talk him through this—just mentioning it and asking him to close his eyes will bring the relaxation.

If the Quiet Bunny doesn't help your child relax, you can move to the calm-down room.

• **Express yourself.** Children's behavior sometimes deteriorates because they can't describe exactly how they feel or what's happening to them. And they don't understand how their behavior affects others. Since your child likely can't do this herself, you can express this for her. Try to guess what she is feeling, and put it into words for her. Verbalize how *you* feel about what she's doing. Be calm and clear. Use short, simple sentences. It's even okay to tell her that you are getting upset—so that you can demonstrate to her what to do with intense emotions by modeling how you handle yours.

• **Tell him what you *do* want.** Instead of focusing on the misbehavior and what you don't want him to do, explain exactly what you'd like your child to do or say instead. Acknowledge your child's feelings, and give him the tools to calm himself and the words to express his emotions. Help your child by demonstrating

Sample Situation	Suggested Parent Response
Your two children are fighting over a toy. They are grabbing it and pushing each other.	You take the toy in hand as you crouch down to their level. Say, "You both want this toy right now, but there is only one toy. Pushing and grabbing isn't a nice way to play. It's better to use your words and make a plan. Would you like me to set the timer so you can each have a turn to play with it, or do you want me to put it away?"
You and your child are in the grocery store, shopping before dinner. He wants a cookie, you say no, and a stream of fussing and whining ensues.	"I know you want a cookie and it's hard when I say no. To grow up strong and healthy you need to eat your nutritious dinner first and a cookie later. Can you ask nicely? Say, 'Mommy, can we buy a cookie and eat it later?'"
Your child wants you to get her a glass of milk and is whining about it.	Get down to your child's level, look her in the eye, and say, "I can't understand you when you use a whining voice. Please use your big-girl voice and say, 'Mommy, may I please have a drink?'"

or modeling exactly what you want to see or hear. Above are three examples.

• **Distract and involve.** Children can easily be distracted when a new or more interesting activity is suggested. If your child is whining or fussing, try viewing it as an "activity" that your child is engaged in. Since children aren't very good multitaskers (they tend to focus on one thing at a time), you might be able to end the unpleasant activity with the recommendation of something different to do. Ignore the fussing for a moment and offer a new activity. For example, if you're in a grocery store and your child is fussing, get his attention and ask, "Can you pick out three nice green apples for me?" If what you're offering sounds more fun than fussing, your child just might take you up on your offer.

- **Invoke her imagination.** If a child is upset about something not going her way, it can help to vocalize her fantasy of what she wishes would happen:

> "I bet you wish we could buy every single toy in this store."
> "Wouldn't it be fun if vegetables were like cookies? I'd say, 'Eat your chocolate chip broccoli!' "
> "I wish we could stay home all day today and build the biggest Lego castle ever!"

Children with active imaginations may take the ball and run with it—expanding on your story and creating the best imaginary outcome. This can often change the total direction of your child's emotional outburst.

- **Use the preventive approach.** Review with your child the desired behavior prior to leaving the house, when entering a public building, or before you begin a play date. This can often prevent the whining or tantrum from even beginning. Put your comments in the positive (tell what you want, not what you don't want) and be specific. Prior to entering a store, you might say, "Eric, we're going into the toy store now. We are going to buy a birthday gift for Troy. We are not buying anything for ourselves today. If you see something you like, let me know and I'll put it on your wish list. I want you to remember to walk beside me, use your quiet voice, and keep your hands to yourself."

- **Make an announcement.** When your child begins talking to you in a whiny, fussy voice, tell her, "When you use your normal voice I will listen to you." Then turn your back to your whining child and make it obvious you are ignoring her by doing a chore or reading a book held in front of your face. If the child continues to whine, repeat the same sequence, without engaging the child any further. (Pleading or discussing will only increase the whining.)

- **Be funny.** Young children can have major meltdowns over the most trivial issues, such as toast cut in the wrong shape or a broken crayon. There is no reason that *you* need to take such matters seriously, though. Of course, you should understand that at that moment your child does truly feel the issue is the most important thing in the world. But here's the good news—it's only the most important thing until the next most important thing comes up. And a funny parent is easily the next most important thing. So lighten up, and try distracting your child with a funny face, silly song, or goofy action. Instead of spiraling down that unpleasant road of whining and tantrums, you'll both feel joy and gladness in its place.

Mother-Speak

"I use the 'Be Funny' approach quite often to stop my daughter's whining and fussing. I found that this tip works wonders for my attitude as well as hers. I use silly voices, tickles, funny faces, and talking stuffed animals to help her calm down. I truly find the laughter helps ease both of our frustrations, and it helps us to transition to a new activity with a refreshing new attitude."

—Renee, mother to Kaylie, age 2, and Alyssa, newborn

- **Allow the fussing!** There are times when your child is fussing because he is unhappy with something you've told him to do or stop doing. If that's the case, it's only fair to let him be sad. After all, you can't truly expect him to be happy that you won't let him have an ice-cream cone, climb on the table, or spend another hour playing at the park!

If your child carries the fussing on long after the issue should be done with, then tell your child that you're going to set the timer for three minutes. She can fuss or whine for three minutes and then she must stop. Some children will complain, "That's not enough time!" If they do, ask, "How much is enough, four or five minutes?" Typically, of course, five will be chosen. Make a big production of setting the timer for five minutes, and announce that she must stop when the timer rings. Most children will stop before the timer rings. If your child doesn't stop after five minutes, you can fall back on one of the other ideas.

> **Mother-Speak**
>
> "I've been so set on never letting my children cry that I have sometimes taken it too far and given in to the fussing so I didn't have to hear them cry. That sometimes just makes things worse. I have learned that sometimes it's okay if they have to cry for a moment if they are unhappy and just trying to get it all out."
>
> **—Christine, mother to Lauren, age 6, and AJ, age 2**

- **Teach.** Often children aren't really aware they are whining, or they don't know exactly what you mean by a tantrum. Have a discussion and demonstrate what this behavior sounds like. (Put on a good show!) Also demonstrate what it sounds like when you use a normal voice. Tell your child you want to help her remember not to whine or have a tantrum, so every time she does this you are going to give her a signal. When she sees the signal she should take a deep breath and find her regular voice. If your signal is somewhat lighthearted it may prevent things from escalating. You might put your fingers in your ears, close your eyes, make a funny face, or take a deep, exaggerated breath yourself to cue her as to what to do next. If you and your child practice the Quiet Bunny, then your signal might be using your hands to make bunny ears, wiggling your nose, or making a little hopping motion.

Mother-Speak

"If Eliot whines, I look directly at him, say nothing, and just raise my eyebrows. The more he whines, the higher my eyebrows go! As soon as he gets the message and asks nicely, he gets what he wants—or at least he gets a polite discussion. This is making progress toward Eliot understanding what whining is and when he is doing it."

—Julie, mother to Eliot, age 3, and Oliver, age 19 months

• **Don't model whining.** Make sure you aren't giving whining lessons. Busy parents often whine about messy rooms, sibling bickering, dawdling children, and, of all things, whining. Check the tone and volume of your own voice and eliminate any whining you might be doing. Children take cues about proper behavior from their parents, and we sometimes send the wrong messages. Being aware of our own actions can help guide us to model the behavior we hope to see in our children.

• **Stop public tantrums.** The same skills we have already covered apply to public tantrums. The biggest issue is for the parent to stay calm and react appropriately, without concern for the audience. Parents' embarrassment over their children's public behavior usually gets in the way of a proper response, which in turn creates a pattern for future expeditions. When you can ignore prying eyes and focus on your child instead, most often the episode will end much, much sooner.

Langston, age 2½

Keep in mind that most public tantrums are caused by underlying emotions such as tiredness, hunger, or frustration. So pinpointing the origin can help you calm your child more quickly.

If public tantrums are a frustrating and regular occurrence, you might want to plan a training session. Say, for example, that every shopping trip involves your child fussing, whining, or having a tantrum. Take your child to the grocery store. Buy a few staples, and put a nice assortment of your child's favorite goodies in the cart (potato chips, ice cream, and cookies). Walk around long enough for the expected misbehavior to occur. Walk the cart over to the register and announce to the cashier that you'll have to leave the groceries and go home because your child is misbehaving. (Smile at the cashier and she'll probably smile back, since she has seen plenty of children having tantrums in the store. She may even have one of her own, so she knows how normal it is!) Then go home. Your child will most likely comment on the loss of the goodies. Just say, "Oh well, some other time." Expect great short-term unhappiness but long-term value!

> ### Mother-Speak
> "When my two-year-old daughter has a public tantrum I try to envision that I'm wearing a sign that says, 'I am an educated, peaceful person; an upstanding citizen; and a loving and devoted mother and wife. There is nothing wrong with ME right now—it's just that my toddler is overheated, hungry, and cranky from missing her nap.' "
>
> **—Jacqueline, mother of Elena, age 2**

- **Don't hold a grudge—when it's over, it's over.** After an episode of misbehavior is finished let it go and move on. Don't feel you must teach a lesson by withholding your approval, love, or company. Children usually bounce right back, and it is okay for you to bounce right back, too.
- **Praise success.** Praise your child's attempts at using a regular voice. "Ariel, I really enjoy hearing your pleasant voice!" Try to say yes to a request made in a regular, polite voice. For example, if your child normally fusses and whines about not having a treat before lunch and today she asks pleasantly, try to give her at least a piece of a cookie to reward her for her appropriate manners. Make sure you tell her why it is okay this time. "Yes, you may have a cookie. I'm saying yes because you asked in such a nice voice and you didn't fuss about it. Lucky you!"
- **Avoid letting your child get tired, hungry, bored, or frustrated.** There are times when you can prevent a child from losing

control of his emotions if you modify the situation that leads up to this. In addition to the chart on pages 108–11, here are some things to keep in mind:

- Keep the same nap time and bedtime seven days a week. A consistent sleep schedule is critical for keeping your child even-tempered throughout the day.
- Feed your child frequently. Children have tiny tummies and need regular nourishment to keep blood sugar levels stable. Five small meals, or three meals plus two healthy snacks, keep a child's moods consistent, much more so than three big meals with long periods between them.
- Give your child toys and games that are geared to his age and ability level.
- Warn your child before changing activities to allow him time to adjust. ("One more swing, then we're going home.")
- Be patient when putting your child in an unfamiliar environment or when introducing him to new people. Don't push him to do what's uncomfortable for him.
- Be prepared. If you expect to run errands all day, or spend time talking with other adults, or stand in long lines, bring along snacks, books, and toys to keep your child occupied.
- Be thoughtful about scheduling. Asking a two-year-old to be pleasant while you spend an entire day on the run is a bit much. Schedule a break, such as a quick stop at the park, when possible.
- Try to be home at nap time and bedtime. Keeping a tired child on the move invites trouble. This can't always be avoided, but steer clear of it when you can!
- Help your child learn new skills before you ask him to do them on his own (such as pouring juice, getting dressed, or working puzzles).

- Keep your expectations realistic; don't expect more than your child is capable of.
- Don't *underestimate* your child's abilities. Allow him the opportunities and privileges that are appropriate for his age.
- As much as possible, keep a regular and predictable schedule to your child's day.
- When your child becomes overly emotional, keep yourself as calm as possible.
- Use a soothing tone of voice, a gentle touch, or the Quiet Bunny to help your child calm down. He can't do it on his own; he needs your help.

Reminder Page

Stop the Tantrums, Fussing, and Whining

- Determine the reason and solve the problem.
- Offer a choice.
- Get eye to eye.
- Validate feelings.
- Let the tantrum run its course.
- Take your child to the calm-down room.
- Do the Quiet Bunny.
- Express yourself—describe and verbalize.
- Tell your child what you DO want.
- Distract and involve.
- Invoke your child's imagination ("I bet you wish . . .").
- Use the preventive approach—review expectations in advance.
- Make an announcement ("Please use a normal voice so I can understand you.").
- Be funny.
- Set a timer and allow fussing for three minutes.
- Teach your child what whining and a tantrum sound like.
- Don't model whining.
- Stop the public tantrums.
- Don't hold a grudge—when it's over, it's over.
- Praise success.
- Avoid letting your child get tired, hungry, bored, or frustrated.

Part 3

A Peaceful Home: Staying Calm and Avoiding Anger

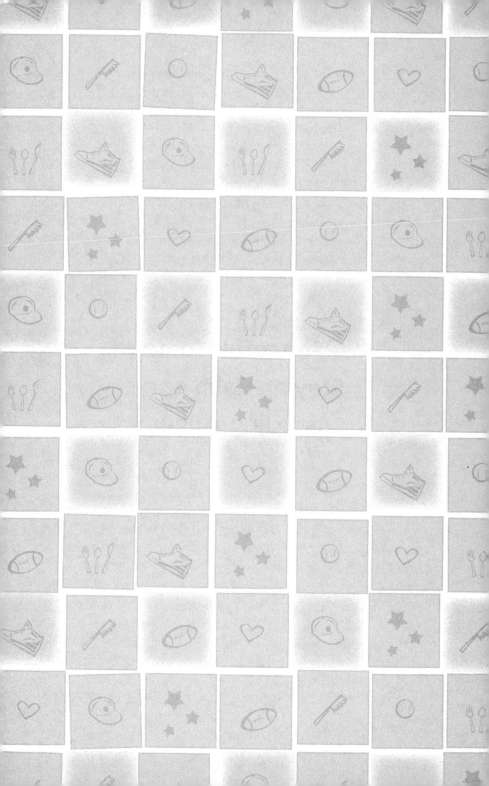

Searching for Peace

Wouldn't it be wonderful if every day of family life were cheerful and relaxed? If our children would always do what they were told (the first time they were told)? And what if we could meet every single adversity with a calm, clear head and then always make the right decisions? As lovely as that sounds, we know that it would be impossible for life to be such a never-ending bowl full of bliss and cherries. It is said that along with cherries come the pits. Anger is an unsightly pit, but it is impossible to avoid it during the child-rearing years.

Family life is complicated and unpredictable. Day-to-day expectations and responsibilities can create angry emotions in parents and children. No matter how skilled you are at parenting, no matter how wonderful your children are, you cannot eliminate or avoid the unpleasant situations that occur in all families. However, once you understand where the anger comes from and learn ways to control your reactions, then anger can occupy a smaller place in your home, one that is manageable and reasonably contained.

Anger

The Shame and the Secret

Our children are so lovable, innocent, and treasured. They bring us incredible joy with just a smile. They love us with their entire beings—and we love them with an intensity that is unique to the parent-child relationship. We'd stand in front of a bus to protect our children—and we'd do it without a second thought. Yet, these same precious children can bring out the worst in us. There are times when they make us so angry that we yell, threaten, condemn, withdraw, or even grab, push, slap, or hit. Afterward, we suffer.

The ferocity and intensity of our anger at our children confuses and frightens us. We think that our actions are wrong, yet we don't know how to control them and so it happens again and again. Each time, we suffer shame and embarrassment over our actions. We don't want to talk about what we did, nor admit that we acted in such a harsh way toward our children. We rationalize, excuse, and blame. And then we suffer in silence. You may think you are the

Mother-Speak

"How do I feel after an angry outburst? I feel guilty, sad, ashamed, embarrassed, disgusted, and depleted. I am flooded with negative self-talk, anguish, worry, and, often, tears. I feel like I've damaged my children. I feel that I am a horrible person and a failure as a mum. Every time it happens, I promise myself I won't do it again. Yet I do."

—**Mother of two**

only one to ever get so unbelievably angry at your own child, and you may feel no one else reacts in such an uncontrolled manner. But I am here to tell you that you are not alone. Far from it. It is likely that every single parent in the entire world—since the beginning of the human race—has erupted in anger at his or her child and has done so more than once. (And even more than twice.)

Being a parent can be the most wonderful experience of a lifetime. Yet, raising children is also one of the most complicated, time-consuming, energy-draining, and challenging tasks you will ever encounter, and anger is a natural outcome of the intensity of the work. Parents who try the hardest to do their best are the ones beset by the most remorse after episodes of anger. So, before we proceed to learn how to understand and control your anger, I'd like to give you permission to abolish the shame and guilt. Rest assured anger happens to everyone. No parent is immune.

Key Point

Anger is as common to parenting as changing diapers. We don't worry about the diapers, and we change them as necessary. However, few of us handle our anger well, and we worry about it too much. The good news is that we *can* learn how to manage and control our anger.

Even though anger at our children is normal and common, it clearly stands in the way of effective parenting. It prevents us from making the right decisions, and it doesn't help us to teach the lessons we want our children to learn. Anger influences how we think, how we behave, and how we live our day-to-day lives. It creates stress and unhappiness for us and for our children. Unresolved and uncontrolled anger can even grow and evolve into a pattern

Mother-Speak

"I've always been great at keeping my cool. I walk away from arguments with my husband because I don't like being angry. I prefer cooling down and talking about it later, another day, or not at all. But, you can't do that with a child. You have to deal with the situation. And, as a consequence, you've got to deal with your anger right now, too. But I'm not sure how to do that. I'm still learning, and every time I get angry, I get embarrassed and ashamed. I'm glad to know that it's normal, both to get angry and also to feel the shame. Perhaps that will alleviate some of the pressure the next time I have to deal with a tantrum."

—Cristina, mother to Maïa, age 3, and Solanne, age 20 months

of behavior that could be potentially dangerous, both emotionally and physically.

The good news is that you can have more control over your emotional states. Once you understand where the anger comes from and you learn specific steps to handle your anger, you will find that it will be a less-intense and less-frequent occurrence in your home, leaving room for positive, effective parenting and loving communication between you and your children.

Why Do Parents Get Angry at Their Children?

It can help to identify the reasons that we get angry at our children. Understanding the underlying causes of anger can be the first step in gaining control of our angry feelings and moving toward prevention and solutions. Let's examine some of the most common sources of parental anger.

Raising Children Is a Difficult, Complex Job That's Always Changing

Parenting is a complicated job that never ends—twenty-four hours, seven days a week, with very few coffee breaks and no vacations. Even when our children are not with us, they often consume our thoughts and energy. It seems we must handle the same problem repeatedly, yet never really solve it. Furthermore, as we master each new stage in our child's development, or as we finally solve the current child-rearing problem, we turn around to find yet another new issue is close on its heels. Any job of this magnitude would invite myriad emotions—including anger.

To make this even more complicated, parenting isn't our only job. Our days are filled with many other obligations that also take up our time and energy, putting even more stress on our shoulders and causing us to be even more short-tempered with our children.

Lack of Adequate Training

Although parenting is a difficult, complex job, it doesn't come with clear instructions. Even if you read parenting books or take classes, every child responds in unique ways and family issues change from day to day. So no matter how prepared you are, it's still all on-the-job training—and the job keeps changing! Because of this, we can never fully "master" parenting, so we often feel as if we're chasing a moving target. Our lack of training for the enormous task can make us insecure and cause us to feel helpless. When trying to force things to go the way we think they should, it can lead us to anger.

Mother-Speak

"Up until a few months ago, I always had control over every aspect of Hannah's life. It was only when she started rebelling that it became clear that she indeed was a separate human being from me with her own set of ideas, preferences, and opinions! Today was the first time it hit me that this shift in behavior and attitude wasn't just about what she wanted to wear or her refusing to listen to me, it was about her starting to be her own person. I think a part of my anger was that I was no longer able to control 'all things Hannah.' It was me being in denial that she is a totally different person from me and that she will most likely be a different person than *I expect and want* her to be. Looks like someone forgot to tell me that when they cut that umbilical cord it meant at some point down the line (two and a half years to be exact) she would start to become a person I would have less and less control over—and whom I'd have to trust would make good choices for herself using the tools that have been taught to her. That brings tears to my eyes . . . partly because I see there is a part of me that doesn't want to believe that one day she *will* fly on her own, when she won't need me as much, and partly because I wish I would have recognized that months ago when my anger and frustration were at its peak.

"The first half of Hannah's twos were a piece of cake. I didn't understand what the big fuss about the terrible twos was all about! Not that Hannah was a perfect angel, but still . . . this second half of the twos has been . . . hmm . . . let's say difficult and interesting. All of a sudden my sweet little girl who always did as she was told and never had a tantrum transformed into a little diva who did what she wanted to do and that was that! The moving target you mentioned was so dead-on. I felt like just when I mastered something and got ahold of a bad behavior, she would change things up and I'd end up flailing! I don't believe in spanking, but I have come really close a couple of times, and that really upset me.

"It helps to see the 'whys' behind the anger, and it has made a big difference already. I am able to stop myself quicker and ask myself where the anger is coming from, and remind myself of her emerging independence—and that it is really a good thing."

—Kia, mother to Hannah, age 2½

Lack of Support

In days past, families were larger, and people tended to stay in the same area their entire lives. Therefore, young parents had grandparents, aunts, uncles, cousins, siblings, and friends close by to help them in their new role as parents. When a problem occurred, there were many people to turn to for help. With today's much smaller family units and increased mobility, extended family members don't live close by; they may even live on different continents. Frequent moves mean that close friendships are harder to maintain.

In addition, many families are headed by one parent only, giving that person the responsibility for all parenting and household duties in addition to the burden of financially supporting the family. This lack of support and added pressure opens the door to much more stress and anger.

Mother-Speak

"Today's parents have pressure on them to function as great parents without the necessary 'scaffolding' to do the job. They lack support, experienced advice, and people just being there to call on. It can be a lonely and difficult job."

—Jane, mother to Isla, age 5, and Willow, age 3

Frustration, Confusion, and Disappointment

Because of the many pressures we just talked about, things in the household don't always go smoothly or according to plan. We can attempt to use every parenting skill in our repertoire, we can have well-planned routines, and we can be thoughtful and even wise, yet we can still end up with children who don't do what we want them to do. This can lead us to feel confused and frustrated—*Why won't my child behave? Why on earth can't I get a handle on this?* It can also cause us to be disappointed in our children and in ourselves as parents. All these negative emotions can easily lead to anger.

We further pump up the volume on our anger with emotional tunnel vision. We see, hear, and understand nothing beyond that which is creating our anger, thus magnifying it beyond actual proportion, building our frustration, confusion, and disappointment into a mountain too big to move.

Unrealistic Expectations

There are three situations where expectations can become out of sync with real life. The first of these is our overall vision for family life. Parents often begin painting a picture of *family* in their mind's eye before their child is even born. During pregnancy or the adoption process, parents will daydream about their future family. This daydreaming focuses on the expected joys of parenthood,

Tristan, age 2½

rarely including the unpleasant or mundane—which make up a significant part of real life. Reality often begins to take a sharp turn away from expectations right from the start—a rough birth, postpartum blues, a delayed adoption, sleepless nights, a colicky baby, and so on.

Another area where expectations go awry has to do with daily discipline and behavior situations. Although we've seen a multitude of children throwing tantrums in our lifetime, although we've witnessed children talking back to their parents, although

Mother-Speak

"When my oldest was two, I was pregnant with our second child. One day, we went out for a walk and she insisted on bringing her riding toy. The only place for her to ride was a good ten-minute walk from our apartment, so I told her that I would let her bring it—on the condition that she ride the whole time and that I didn't have to carry it. Of course she said yes. Of course she rode the whole way there, and of course she got tired and refused to ride back. At this point I should have realized that I was expecting *way* too much of my little girl, but I was so absorbed with my own exhaustion that I got extremely annoyed at her. I picked up her toy and lectured her the entire way home about responsibility. Yes, I know, that's crazy. She was only two! But I did it anyway. I don't think any memory has ever made me feel quite so stupid before! I guess we really should keep our expectations of our children in step with reality, but in the moment that's not always easy to do."

—Elana, mother to Choshen, age 5; Maayan, age 3; and Shmuel, age 5 months we know that children fuss, whine, and fight, and although each of us *has been* a child who misbehaved, we somehow have in our subconscious mind the expectation that *my child will be different.* We think that if we love our child enough, he'll always love us back by being *good.* So when our child has a tantrum, throws food on the floor, or purposely breaks rules, we are thrown by the vast difference between our expectations and reality.

The last of our skewed expectations has to do with our vision of how we should be as parents. We often set high goals for ourselves without even being aware that we are doing so. We create these goals by viewing our parents, by observing other parents, and by reading or going to classes. We may have hated it when our parents screamed at us and vow never to do the same. We may see other parents beg, threaten, or bribe their children and *know* we will never react that way. We might wholeheartedly agree with the fundamentals of positive parenting techniques and plan to use rational, well-intentioned parenting skills to raise our children. Yet, there are times when we end up screaming, begging, threatening, bribing, and failing miserably at the techniques we so totally believe in.

These discrepancies between expectation and reality create a cavern that is often unwittingly filled with anger. The larger the cavern, the more room there is for anger. In other words, the further reality is from your expectation, the greater the chance that the gap will be filled with anger or other unpleasant emotions.

Life's Irritations Are Misdirected

At times, the anger that we take out on our children has nothing whatsoever to do with them. We may have had an argument with our spouse, a bad day at work, a problem with our computer, or any number of other issues that annoy us. Along comes our child, acting out perhaps in the simplest way, but at the wrong time, and we release all our anger at our unsuspecting child. It's the "kick the cat" syndrome.

At other times, our child may indeed have misbehaved. The misbehavior triggers our *anger* release button—our child's behavior is added to the growing pileup of other angers, which exaggerate and distort our response. So, rather than having an appropriate reaction to the situation at hand, we explode with all our pent-up anger from so many other issues.

Mother-Speak

"When I have my bad days I have to keep reminding myself not to take out my problems on my daughter. I keep telling myself it's really *my* mood that's the problem, more than my child's behavior. So I say in my head over and over again, 'Do not take out your bad mood on Arianna.' It really helps on those bad days."

—Kristi, mother to Arianna, age 30 months

Anger Is Masking Other Emotions

Human beings are complex creatures. The emotions we show are not always what they seem to be. There are times when what we truly feel is hidden but what escapes to the world is anger. There are times when anger masks other emotions such as worry, fear, embarrassment, frustration, or helplessness, such as when your child disappears at the grocery story (worry), runs into the street (fear), has a tantrum in public (embarrassment), continues his misbehavior no matter what we do (frustration), or is disrespectful and mean to others (helplessness). The anger that erupts in these cases prevents us from acknowledging the painful emotions that are at the root of the situation and can even be a disguised cry of distress.

Mother-Speak

"I think that anger is sometimes associated with our own fears of adequacy. I feel frustration and anger when my child misbehaves in public or around friends or family members. Sometimes it is so hard to handle a situation when you feel the stares of those around you. You fear what they are going to think of your parenting. Even though it shouldn't matter, many times it does."

—Anne-Marie, mother of Lindsey, age 4

It's a Normal Emotional Response to Problems

Human beings have a wide range of emotions, and anger is one of them. To be human is to experience a flow of emotions in response to internal stimulus and external events. All people get angry. It is a natural, biological response to pain (physical or emotional), threats, and frustration. Anger inspires powerful, focused, single-minded behaviors that are necessary for people to defend themselves when they are in dangerous situations. At those times, anger is a necessary human survival mechanism. The problem, of course, is that anger is not perfectly selective; we get angry in situations that don't truly call for anger.

Miles, age 4

Your natural personality traits will also dictate how mad you get and how easily you are set off. Some people are more easily angered than others, and everyone handles their emotions differently. Some people shout, some strike out, some become irritable. Some turn their anger inward as they simmer and sulk, even becoming ill with headaches, stomachaches, or worse.

Keep in mind also that our moods affect our responses to our children. On a good day, when we our mood is cheerful, a spilled cereal bowl is just a spill. On a difficult day, in a bad mood, it's an intentionally created disaster. We aren't perfect beings, and we should never expect perfection of ourselves, just as we shouldn't expect our children to be perfect angels every day.

We can learn to identify, manage, and control our angry feelings so that our reactions don't escalate out of control and make

> **Key Point**
>
> Anger itself cannot be eliminated, nor need it be. Anger is not the real problem. The problem is in how we respond when we are angry.

situations worse than they already are. We can learn to use anger as a cue that something is wrong and needs to be changed. We can, in fact, turn angry emotions into a launching pad for practical problem solving.

Trying to NOT Get Angry

When your child throws an Olympic-sized tantrum at the shopping mall, paints on the sofa, spills juice on your computer, or hits his baby sister, the natural, automatic, and inevitable response is anger. Some people advise against hording anger and tell you to let it loose. But psychologists tell us that this is a dangerous belief as it can escalate anger and possibly lead to aggression. It also can prevent finding a solution to the real problem.

Instead of trying *not* to get angry—which is nearly impossible—or holding your anger in (which can backfire in other ways), it would be better to focus on *identifying* your emotions *and properly responding* to the situation at hand. In other words, the more you try not to be angry in anger-producing situations, the more likely your emotions will explode out of control.

The goal is to develop and practice strategies that allow you to deal with your angry feelings in ways that protect other people and things, while leading you to the proper resolution for the problem.

Mother-Speak

"If I am tired, hungry, rushed, or stressed out, I can't seem to call up even the simplest parenting technique and I find any bit of childish behavior unbearable. I am likely to snap with orders and demands. I have even lashed out with a slap on a leg or hand, which has left me feeling horrified and dismayed with myself. Because this is so far from how I choose to parent, I find it very shameful and distressing. And, of course, I feel guilty and afraid that I have damaged our relationship or even damaged my child's psyche in some way. My own parents were not spankers, but when pushed to the limit my mom did reach out and pinch legs or buttocks. I can see myself reacting to irritation and frustration in the same way. So I guess I should be thankful that I had good parents who were not actually violent, as it must be very hard to break that cycle. It is very clear to me that violence and even anger do absolutely nothing to help my child, and they certainly don't help me. So I am eager to find more ways to control them. I wish I would have been taught how to express anger in a constructive way and then find a way to cool off and get on with things more positively."

—Amy, mother to Amani, age 20 months

Lack of Anger Management Skills

It's possible that no one has ever taught you any specific skills for handling your anger constructively. It's not likely your parents taught you as a child, and it's not a class taught at school. Even worse, you may have learned poor anger management approaches from experiences with your own parents and other people who influenced your emotional growth. Children (and you were one, once) often copy the behavior of other people in their lives, and this applies to how they see angry emotions dealt with. With time, what children observe becomes their own pattern of behavior and will remain so, even up through adulthood, unless they take action to modify their normal responses.

Typically the only adults who take anger management classes are those who are in family or marriage therapy or those who are ordered by a court of law to do so because of extreme anger problems. This is truly a shame, since every human being could benefit from learning anger management skills. In the following pages, you will learn specific skills for controlling parental anger as well as tips on how to teach your children these valuable life skills.

One other point to keep in mind is that all people respond to tense situations differently, and we all have different "angry" personalities. Some people yell, others stomp, some sulk or escape from the person they are mad at. It can help to think about how you automatically respond when you are angry—what are your typical thoughts and actions? If you identify and understand what your automatic responses are, then you will have more power to change those actions.

Self-Neglect, Pain, or Exhaustion

It's common for parents to be stressed and constantly busy. They tend to their children's needs with rarely a moment to themselves. They don't eat right, they don't exercise, and they don't get enough sleep. While unaware of what is happening, this constant caregiving and self-neglect can build into a subconscious resentment and an unmet need for personal space. These buried emotions can be pushed to the surface. Fueled by daily parenting frustrations, they can erupt in a moment of anger.

Busy parents must continue to function no matter how they feel. Tending to children, running a household, and working a job keep us busy from sunup to sundown, and often throughout the night as well, tending to a sleepless child. Parents must push on through sleep-deprivation or pain, including headaches, backaches, head colds, symptoms of pregnancy, postpartum depression, or other discomforts. Human beings have a natural tendency to have a shorter fuse when dealing with their own physical problems.

Children, of course, don't understand or comprehend their parents' pains. So they continue with their normal whining, bickering, or nagging—and push a suffering parent past patience. Even innocent, happy play that is noisy or rambunctious can trigger an angry response from a parent who is dealing with pain or exhaustion. Parents who are under the influence of drugs (both medications and recreational drugs) or alcohol will find their normal emotions to be skewed, which can result in angry responses.

Repeated episodes of uncalled-for anger can cause inconsistent, confusing behavior that can interfere with good discipline practices and damage the parent-child relationship.

Lack of Motivation to NOT Get Angry

You *can* control your anger. You *do* control your anger all the time. Don't believe me? Think of the times that you've been upset with a store clerk, restaurant server, superior at work, neighbor, government official, or driver in front of you. How many times did you swallow that anger and respond in a civilized manner? Think of times that your child misbehaved but you held your anger because the situation occurred in public or in front of your boss, mother-in-law, minister, or child's teacher. You were able to control your anger in all of these situations because there would have been a social price to pay if you had responded angrily. You might have suffered damage to your reputation, embarrassment, shame, or, worse, a fine or arrest.

When you get angry at your child, the worst thing that you perceive happening in return is your child's anger or tears. While this is never a desirable outcome, it's not enough to stop you in your tracks. This is not a conscious decision, but it happens nonetheless.

Once you acknowledge that anger is not an effective parenting response and that it can damage your relationship with your child, while other methods will actually bring positive long-term results, you will be more motivated to learn a method for controlling your outbursts. When that happens, you will learn, practice, and adopt methods that prevent you from releasing your anger in favor of better, more effective responses.

Noise, Disorganization, Mess, and General Chaos

Most of us have a picture in our minds of how we'd like our homes to run. We envision orderly belongings, smooth schedules, and peaceful surroundings. (Should I add chocolate chip cookies baking in the oven?) The reality is that most of our homes have far more noise, mess, and chaos than we would like. Often we live

Father-Speak

"Bad day at work, sales calls, things breaking, noise, headache . . . it all leads to stress that leads to ARGHHHHH!"

—Alan, father to Leanne, age 3, and Timothy, age 5 months

with it day after day after day while wishing it were different. Then, one day when the TV is blaring and the baby is crying, you trip over a stray toy, discover a broken dish, or are startled by a loud and annoying screech. Suddenly all your unhappiness comes pouring out at once.

It can help to know and accept that while there are children in your house it will never make the cover of *Better Homes and Gardens*. Decide on what's most important, set a routine, and relax your standards to protect your sanity. When your children grow up and leave the nest, then your house will look exactly the way you'd like: clean, neat, and organized. And you'll miss them so much you'll wonder why you ever made such a big deal about the clutter.

Children Are Childish

Children are inexperienced, naïve, and narcissistic. They have limited knowledge about social rules and expected behavior. Furthermore, they are separate people from us and they have free will. As hard as you may try, you cannot *make* a child eat, sleep, pick up his toys, say please, or go potty. You can ask. You can nag, plead, threaten, and beg, but your child is a separate human being and functions independently from you. Children are not wise, rational, or mature. They want to do what they want to do, and they don't give much thought to the past or the future, let alone how their actions affect other people or things.

Children don't always understand things the way we assume that they do. We might think that they have learned a lesson, or we might assume that they clearly understand a request, but many times they *don't get it*. This can be very frustrating to parents who think that something is clear as a bell, yet their child is going off in an entirely different direction.

Jordan, age 3

We can't force children to be less childish, and we can't hurry the process of their growing up. And if we think about it, we wouldn't want to, because the same limits that frustrate us bring us the most joy—watching our child's joyful, unrestrained approach to the world is endearing. However, when this juvenile existence means that our children don't, won't, or can't do something we want them to do, and we can't find a way to *make them* do it, then parental anger is the inevitable result.

Wow! There Are Lots of Reasons for Parental Anger!

Now that you've learned the many, many reasons that parents get angry, you may begin to wonder how you ever get through a day without being angry! It is a major feat to stay calm in light of the many plates we must juggle and the many negative issues that are thrown our way. So, yes, give yourself a pat on the back for every issue that you handle with aplomb. And now, let's begin building your knowledge and your anger management skills up so that you'll know exactly what to do next time you find yourself getting angry with your child.

Different Levels of Anger

Anger is a term that defines a broad range of emotions from mild irritation to rage. Not all of these emotions are bad or dangerous. Less intense emotions can act as a motivation to seek change and an impetus to find problem-solving solutions. Lesser degrees of angry emotions keep us focused and keep our children "on their toes." These emotions, such as displeasure or irritation, can allow us to see that a problem exists, but they don't thwart control over our actions. As emotions become more extreme, though, they become harder to control and are more likely to result in uncontrolled reactions with no positive outcome.

> **Key Point**
> A raised voice is not necessarily a bad thing—if it is controlled and respectful.

One problem with anger is that if you don't have control over your emotions at the start you can unintentionally escalate from mild anger to more extreme emotions, bypassing the point where you can use your emotions in a positive way. In addition, the angrier the parent gets, the more out of control the child gets—it's as if they are on two sides of a rolling snowball heading for a crash at the bottom of the mountain. An escalating range of angry emotions might look like this:

Level 1	Level 2	Level 3	Level 4	Level 5	Level 6
Displeasure	Annoyance	Irritation	Exasperation	Rage	Fury

Parental anger often starts out on the mild end of this emotion scale but can build to an uncontrollable crescendo. The following chart shows how this can happen.

How a Parent's Angry Emotions Can Escalate Out of Control

Child's Action	Parent's Action	Parent's Emotion
Plays with toys	Notes that it is bedtime and asks child to put toys away: "Time to get ready for bed."	Calm
Hears but ignores parent, continues to play with toys	Notes child's inaction and repeats request: "Didn't you hear me? Put your toys away."	Displeased
Puts one toy away, but brings out two more and begins to play with them	Sees time is getting later but child is still playing; pleads with child: "Get busy! Time to clean up!"	Annoyed
Complains and begs for more playtime	Demands obedience: "Do it NOW!"	Irritated
Whines and fusses	Raises voice and threatens punishment: "Just stop whining and clean up or no storytime!"	Exasperated (Upset)
Falls to floor crying, ignoring toys scattered around him	Yells at child and begins to throw toys in toy box: "Why can't you just do what I say!! You make me so mad!"	Rage-filled

Child's Action	Parent's Action	Parent's Emotion
Grabs toys out of toy box, stomps feet, and cries	Loses control, spanks child, and drags him to his bedroom while shouting at him: "I am tired of this! Get to bed, NOW!"	Furious
Cries to sleep in bed, feeling unloved and confused	Feels frustrated, guilty, and ashamed	Regretful

You can see how emotions can escalate between parent and child. Parents can avoid this escalation when they learn how to identify anger at the milder levels and make precise choices about how to respond to the angry feelings. Going one step further, parents can also learn how to communicate to the child in ways that encourage cooperation. Before we move on to those skills, we'll examine *why* and *how* angry emotions grow in their intensity.

Your Anger

Do You Accidentally Make Things Worse?

Many parents unwittingly feed and grow their anger. As anger begins to grow inside you, it prevents rational thoughts—it shuts off the thinking part of your brain. The thoughts that begin to run rampantly through your head are inaccurate and irrational and based on mistaken beliefs. You view situations as final and definitive and see your child's actions as intentionally bad rather than seeing what's happening as part of the natural process of raising children.

Let's examine some of the common mistaken beliefs and negative thoughts that cause angry emotions to spiral out of control. Then we'll adjust the beliefs to reflect a more accurate way of thinking.

My Children Should Never Misbehave, So When They Do They Make Me Angry

You probably read that sentence and thought, *Well, of course that's not true!* Your rational, calm state of mind allows you to understand that. However, when you are in the midst of an episode of misbehavior you may shake your head in bafflement at your child's actions and wonder what is wrong with him, or what's wrong with you. In reality, there is nothing wrong with him, or with you, either. Children misbehave. Parents have the job of teaching their child how to behave appropriately. If children were born knowing how to behave in all situations, they wouldn't need parents, would they?

Here is the unexpected and hidden concept behind the second half of this mistaken belief—that when our children misbehave they *make us angry*. It is *not* our child's misbehavior that makes us angry because a child's actions cannot *make* you feel or do *anything*. You are in control of your feelings and your actions. Therefore, you actually allow the anger to formulate. You create your own anger by the way you interpret your child's behavior. You are not alone here, as this is the foundation for much parental anger. Here's an important first step to anger control: You must accept responsibility for your own anger.

> **Key Point**
> My child's misbehavior does not cause my anger. I create anger by my interpretation of the behavior and with my response to that interpretation.

You may find that learning more about child development and what behaviors are normal at your child's age will help you to avoid labeling actions as misbehavior when they are actually age-appropriate behavior. There are plenty of books available about normal child development. They outline typical and expected behaviors and describe usual characteristics of certain age groups. You can also learn what's normal by talking with parents who have children close in age to your own, by reading parenting magazines, or by discussing your concerns with your pediatrician or family health care provider.

By understanding normal development, you may even be able to avoid the problem altogether—at times. As an example, if you know that young children are prone to temper tantrums when they are tired and hungry and your child has a meltdown thirty minutes before dinner on the day that he misses his nap, you can identify the cause and understand the resulting behavior. This doesn't mean that you'll accept or ignore the behavior, but you will find it easier to handle than if you interpret the act as your child's personality problem or a deficiency in your parenting skills. Furthermore, you may be able to sometimes prevent it from happening.

I Shouldn't Have to Repeat Myself Over and Over Again on the Same Issue

Human beings are not created to learn things instantly upon the first lesson. This is true for children and adults. Students must study, college classes have reviews, baseball teams have practices, and orchestras, dancers, and actors have rehearsals. As they say, practice makes perfect. Children have an incredible amount of things to learn in their lives, and they don't easily transfer lessons learned from one area to another. For example, they may learn not to run into the street but not understand that they also shouldn't run into a parking lot. Your toddler might learn not to touch the TV controls but still reach for the DVD controls or the computer keyboard. There is an almost endless amount of new input in the early years. It's a lot to process and remember.

This concept is complicated by the fact that even when children learn a rule, it doesn't mean that they will always abide by it! This applies to family rules, societal rules, and rules of nature. Children will often test to see if the rules still hold true, or if they can manage to bend them or even break them without any repercussions. Children may believe they have a good reason to break the rule. They might think the rule is unfair, or they might think no one is watching so they can't get caught, or they may not understand the rule or how it applies to the situation. One other reason is that the forbidden is too enticing to resist.

Mother-Speak

"I'm eight months' pregnant, so my two-year-old can be a bit of a challenge to keep up with. Yesterday, I was tired and we were at bath-and-bedtime. She was obviously getting tired herself and melting down a bit, so I asked her to pull out the plug and come out of the tub. She pulled the plug, but absolutely refused to get out. She actually lay down in the tub, as the water drained around her. I can't bend over and pick her up from that angle, so I got totally frustrated. I said, 'Fine. Don't get out. Stay in there. I can't do this anymore.' I sat down on the chair near the tub, hung my head, and wouldn't look at her. She stood up and said, 'Mommy, can I give you a kiss and make you feel better?' Wow, I sure did feel better in a hurry!

"Sometimes it's so hard to step back and realize that this is a little PERSON I'm dealing with. She has her own thoughts and ideas and plans—she's not out to make me miserable. Sometimes it just takes a kiss to clear our heads again and make it all better!"

—Sheri, mother to Faith, age 2½

Actually, adults still engage in this rule-testing behavior: Do you always obey the posted speed limit? No? According to some studies, almost 70 percent of drivers admit to speeding over the posted limit. You might speed on a given day because

- You're in a rush to make it to an appointment. (You have a good reason.)
- You think the limit is too slow for the road. (The rule is unfair.)
- You know there's never a police car on the road. (You won't get caught.)

- You didn't see the speed limit sign. (You didn't know the rule.)
- Your new car *needs* to go fast. (It was too tempting to resist.)

You can increase the odds that your child will learn rules by keeping them simple and specific, and then being very consistent in enforcing them.

My Child Misbehaves Just to Spite Me

When your child is misbehaving, pushing your buttons, and totally out of control, you may think, *Why is she doing this to me?* In reality, your child isn't even thinking about you at all, except to the extent that you are standing in the way of what she wants to do. Children don't misbehave just to make you mad—they don't want to hear you yell and they don't want to be punished — they would avoid that at all costs! Your child wants what she wants, when she wants it—it's as simple as that.

My Child Listens to Me Only When I Get Angry

Many parents believe this to be true because it *has been true* for them. The reason for this is that some parents only get serious about discipline when they become angry. In my book *Hidden Messages: What Our Words and Actions Are Really Telling Our Children*, I tell the story of a parent affected by this dilemma:

> Ken is sitting at the kitchen table handling his least favorite task—filling out tax forms. He's surrounded by checkbooks, calculator, paperwork, and his cup filled with coffee. His children, Katie and Andy, are happily playing a game close by in the family room. All is quiet

on this Saturday morning—at least until two high-pitched giggling fits abruptly break the silence.

Ken peers over his glasses at the source of the merriment. "Hey guys, I'm *working* in here." The room settles into quiet again, but not for long. Game pieces suddenly find lives of their own, their rambunctious activities narrated by two young voices. Not even glancing their way, Ken grumbles, "You guys are being awfully noisy." The pieces continue their action in a whisper, and Ken again focuses on his work.

Not five minutes later, the game pieces engage in a mock-battle that ends in a loud crescendo. Ken expresses his exasperation in two words: "Katie! Andy!" He shakes his head and mumbles, "Why don't these kids ever listen to me?" He begins, once again, to wade through the endless tax forms. Just as the instructions start to make sense, his energetic young ones, now bored by their fantasy play, begin a new game, complete with shouts and whooping around the room.

Ken's patience reserve has been depleted—and to signal the event, he slams his pencil on the table, scrapes back his chair, and marches into the family room and up to the children. With a bright red face and bulging eyes, he bellows, "Katherine Nicole! Andrew Shawn! I have had *enough*! I cannot work with all the noise! Either BE QUIET or GO OUTSIDE and play!"

The kids mutter, "Sorry, Daddy," as they shuffle out of the room and head for the swing set in the backyard. Ken walks back to the table, his hands nervously combing back his hair, his breath labored. He's wondering why his kids only listen to him when he gets angry.

When you examine this situation you'll see what really happened. This father lacks purpose or skill at the beginning of the story. He makes his first three statements from another room with no specific instructions or call to action. He makes vague comments without telling the children what he wants from them. (What exactly is the right response to "Hey guys, I'm *working* in here"? Maybe, "Good for you, Daddy. Someone has to pay taxes around here.") It isn't until Ken gets angry that he actually uses good parenting skills! One—he walks into the room and faces his children directly. Two—he states the problem. "I cannot work with all the noise." Three—he gives them a solution: a choice they all can live with. "Either be quiet or go outside and play."

In essence, Ken's anger was not necessary, and it wasn't anger that solved the problem. It was the three specific parenting skills he unknowingly used. However, if Ken continues this pattern, his children will learn that he only means business when he gets angry, so he may unwittingly fall into a pattern of angry parenting.

My Angry Outbursts Create Permanent Damage in Our Relationship

Nearly all parents love their children with an intensity that matches nothing else on earth. Their children are a part of their heart and soul, and the center of their lives. So when parents erupt in anger at their children, they feel they have created a permanent hole in the relationship, as test mom Bridget expresses in the story that follows.

Of course, a parent's rage, physical aggression, or hurtful words can create holes. Repeated hostility as well as violent words and actions can leave a lasting mark on a child's personality. It's very important to learn how to control your anger to prevent it from reaching this danger zone. However, we should not worry quite so much that every angry moment leaves its mark. Most of our outbursts are simply moments of unpleasantness that can be overcome with constructive parenting skills. Love and positive interaction can make up for bad moments in an otherwise good relationship—kind of like a quality putty and some paint can touch up that fence. Children are a great deal more resilient than fences—the little holes usually fill right up with the next hug and giggle.

Mother-Speak

"Whenever I think about anger, it reminds me of a story I heard. It's the one about the boy who would have these angry outbursts, and every time he did, his father would have him hammer a nail into their fence. During a calmer moment, he had his son take out all the nails he had hammered into the fence. There were big holes where the nails had been, marring the fence. His father said that every time he had one of those angry outbursts, it had a permanent effect on the people around him, just like those unsightly holes in the fence. This story always fills me with tremendous guilt because I do realize that my children absorb my angry outbursts and I feel like I am leaving those holes behind."

—Bridget, mother to Ethan, age 7; Devan, age 3; and Sage, age 19 months

Having a Plan to Manage Your Anger

Now you understand that as a parent you *are* going to get angry at your child *and* you can't change that fact. However, you can change what you do with that anger when it first appears, and you can learn how to stop it from growing out of control.

It is nearly impossible to rein in your emotions at the time they occur *unless you have a plan in advance.* Having an anger plan is like leaving for a road trip with a map and driving directions to follow versus having no plan and driving off with a general destination in mind, but no specifics on how to get there. Once you are on the road you are moving forward, but without a specific plan you may never reach your destination. The same analogy applies to anger. When it catches you off guard, it likely takes off with a life of its own. If you have a plan, however, you can direct your emotions in the way that suits your goals as a parent.

The Danger of Anger

There are a few things that should occur in order for you to be able to make the best use of the six-step plan to staying calm, which will be described later. First, you must believe that no good comes from anger. Anger, in and of itself, is not a solution to any problem. It often makes things worse by causing your child to focus on your harsh words and actions. Children have natural defensive responses to a parent's anger: they feel misunderstood, attacked, or unfairly accused. Whether these are true or accurate beliefs does not matter—they still prevent a child from learning the lesson you

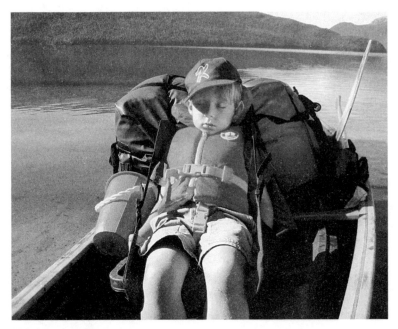

Stanley, age 4½

are trying to impart, and in the worse cases, when repeatedly used, drive a wedge between parent and child.

The other important idea to accept is that almost any problem can be held off for a time, until you gain control of yourself. It's a rare parenting issue that requires an instant response or solution. Even a young child has enough memory power to remember what he or she did an hour or more after it happened. (If you don't believe me, test the idea. While you're preparing dinner, promise your child that you'll go out for ice cream after you eat—and see if your promise is remembered!)

In most cases, when you can halt anger, collect yourself, and then approach the issue with a level head, you will have much better results than if you fly off the handle and explode in anger. Children usually don't learn the intended lesson from an angry parent.

However, they can learn valuable lessons when a controlled parent makes a specific discipline decision.

Another reason why it is important to manage your anger effectively is because repeated, uncontrolled anger can cause a parent to resort to physical punishment. Such punishments as spanking, slapping, or pinching a child have all been proven to be ineffective and potentially harmful methods of discipline. Repeated anger can also lead to major family problems, such as child abuse, divorce, or mental health problems for parents and children, including depression or anxiety.

Once you view anger as a potentially dangerous emotion that is wise to avoid, you need to be able to recognize when anger is happening to you. As we discussed previously, there are many stages of anger, from mild to extreme. The sooner you acknowledge that your emotions are creeping up the anger scale the better, since it's much, much easier to gain control at the start.

You can start to learn how to control your anger by tuning into your body and feeling the anger rising within you. While everyone feels emotions differently, there are a number of typical physical signs that accompany anger. Next time you begin to feel angry, try to note which of these early warning signs of anger you feel:

- Clenched teeth
- Tight jaw
- Tense body
- Shallow, rapid breathing
- Tight stomach, stomach pains, or nausea
- Increased heart rate
- Heated face, neck, or ears
- Tightened muscles
- A feeling of pounding or fullness in the head, similar to a headache
- Sweating

- Shaking
- Squinting
- A change in tone or volume of voice
- The need to curse or say harsh words
- The urge to scream or cry
- The urge to hit, slam things, bang things, or run away
- An inability to hear or understand others

Learning to recognize your own early warning signs of anger allows you to rein in your temper. When we begin to metamorphose into our angry self, much of our behavior becomes automatic and harder to control.

What Triggers Your Anger?

It is helpful to identify those things that provoke your anger so you are aware of the possibility of anger before it even begins. You can also examine the issue in advance—at a time when you are calm and in control—to see what changes you can make to stop the incidents from occurring. This allows you to use preventive action that will change your child's behavior, which in turn reduces the amount of anger that you might feel.

As an example, let's say that your children argue when seated beside each other in the car. The arguing, while you are trying to drive, is distracting and frustrating. You usually end up yelling at the pair of them. Since you are in the vehicle two or more times every day, this is a major anger issue in your life. So instead of going about things in exactly the same way and getting exactly the same results, take time to plan how to solve the problem. You might post "car rules" with exact consequences for breaking them. You might put books, lap games, and snacks in the car to keep the children busy and happy. You might create a chart to log successes in the car so that your children can earn a reward for staying pleasant in the car. By approaching this anger trigger in a productive way, you can reduce the amount of arguments that occur in the car, thus reducing the amount of anger in your day. This technique can be used for any issue that repeatedly triggers your anger.

Most parents get angry about issues that are insignificant in the grand scheme of life, yet happen on such a regular basis that the issues become blown way out of proportion. So take the time to identify your anger triggers. Then, perhaps using the skills in this book, set a plan to correct each behavior problem that sets off your anger. There are common parenting issues that trigger anger.

- Backtalk
- Constant interruptions when you're busy
- Ignoring a parent's calls or requests
- Lack of cooperation
- Procrastination and dawdling
- Refusing to do as told
- Repeated misbehavior that doesn't cease
- Sibling bickering and fighting
- Temper tantrums
- Unacceptable behavior in public (such as public tantrums/not cooperating)
- Unnecessary crying
- Whining

In addition to triggers like these, there are "hot spots" or danger zones in the day when anger more easily rises to the surface. These are typically times when family members are tired, hungry, or stressed, and those emotions leave us more vulnerable to anger.

- Mornings, when rushing to get to work and/or school
- Mid-day, when children and parents have a dip in energy, older kids come home from school, and no one has had a nap

- When your home is filled with playmates or visitors
- Immediately after work when the day's stresses are still brewing
- Before dinner, when everyone is hungry and dealing with end-of-the-day tension
- Late evening, just before bedtime, when everyone is tired

Key Point

Doing things the way you've always done them and expecting different results only leaves you frustrated and angry. Instead, identify your anger triggers and daily hot spots and take action to change things for the better.

It can help to look over the previous lists and determine what your triggers and hot spots are. Once you identify them, think about what you can do differently to ward off some of those things that spark your anger. For example, if the morning rush brings too much stress, you can prepare the night before by setting out clothing, packing lunches, and collecting shoes and coats. Create a "morning routine poster" that outlines the morning routine step-by-step. If you find that tempers are short in the hour before dinner, then set out healthy appetizers, such as vegetables with dip or cheese and fruit, and note if this helps. If your children bicker about sharing toys, set up specific rules for sharing, label special toys that aren't available for sharing, teach the new rules to your children, and enforce them quickly when they aren't obeyed.

It helps to keep in mind all of the reasons for parental anger and the mistaken beliefs that we covered earlier. When you train yourself to look for the underlying problems, you will become more aware of them. When you become aware of these underlying reasons for your anger, you will be more likely to control your emotions before they explode.

Anger is not something that can be dealt with once and then it will go away! As your children grow and change and as new issues appear, you'll find yourself needing a reminder of all that you have learned. So, reread these pages from time to time for a quick refresher course. That way you can take a fresh look at the issues that create negative emotions in your family and refresh your memory about how to manage anger.

Mother-Speak

"I often find that I am talking to a brick wall with my two-year-old daughter. She wants what she wants, and she doesn't like to do what she's being asked to do. Her responses to things I want from her are either silence, ignoring me, or continuing to whine and cry, and it infuriates me until I yell at her. However, I have come to realize that when I get mad at her she thinks that somehow my love for her has lessened. Nowadays, when we have an episode of defiance and an exchange afterward, I don't let it linger. I pick her up and hug her. She lays her head on my shoulder, and I remind myself that she is a cherished child.

"Only a few years ago, I had no child to hold and thought I'd never have one. How quickly I forgot how much pain I was in from not having a child! And here I am, getting upset at her little antics; the behavior that would be so welcomed in the life of a childless woman. I realize that I am truly blessed. She is a joy to hold and to love. I have to make a conscious effort to remember that after all she is only a little child."

—Shaila, mother to Aanayh, age 2½

And, finally, hold on to the feeling of love that is the foundation of your relationship with your child. Take time every day to bask in the joy of being a parent. Take time to play. Take time to talk and listen. Hug, kiss, and cuddle your children often. When you build up this foundation of positive love and emotion, you will find yourself less likely to experience intense anger.

Now it's time to move on to the specific six-step process that you can use to control your anger.

Your Anger Control Plan: Six Steps to Staying Calm

The following six-step process can be used to curb your anger whenever you feel your child pushing your buttons. Actually, it can be used in any life situation when you find your angry emotions getting the better of you. It is a process that takes time and effort to master, yet it is definitely well worth the effort. You may wish to post the summary found on page 188 in a convenient place for handy reference. Once you have practiced and are experienced with the steps you'll no longer need the printed reminder. It may become the *new* natural way you handle your angry emotions.

Step 1: Stop

Step 1 toward gaining control is to stop yourself as soon as you realize you are getting angry. The purpose is to catch yourself at the very start of your anger and stop your emotions from escalating out of control.

When your anger controls your words and actions, what follows will be unpleasant and ineffective. You will *not* teach your child what you intend to teach. He or she will not hear the meanings of your words—instead your child will be mired in your anger. Your

Spencer, age 2

child's focus will be your anger, not whatever point you are trying to make. If you stop and wait, however, you can make your point and teach a better lesson. When you are calm and in control you can be rational and achieve the goal you are setting out for.

It's a fact of life that you are going to get upset, annoyed, and frustrated with your child, and you are going to raise your voice. A short burst of unhappiness that quickly dissipates is not an issue to be concerned with. However, the minute you no longer feel in control of your words or actions, the situation begins to go downhill fast and all hope of teaching is lost.

As you sense your control slipping—STOP. If you are in the middle of a sentence—STOP—don't even finish your thought, except perhaps to say, "I'm getting mad!" If you are moving—STOP moving. Practice a STOP gesture that can be used as a way to put a physical brake on your emotions, and also as a signal to your child that your anger is rising out of control. A good STOP gesture is to hold your hands up in front of your face, fingers straight up, palms out. Push the anger away from you, and at the same time say the word *stop*. You can say it loudly and firmly. Combining the action and the word has two purposes. It is a physical motion to help you halt your actions, and it is directed at your child to let him know you are too angry to continue.

This stop is for *you*. It is not intended to stop your child's actions because it most likely will not stop your child's misbehavior. Your yelling child may continue to yell. Your tantruming child might continue to tantrum. Your bickering children might continue to bicker. The theory here is that you must get yourself calmed down in order to deal with your child's misbehavior. If you are lucky, over time, this may begin to stop your child's action as well. He or she may learn that once you stop there is no point in continuing, since you will be disengaged.

I recommend that you talk to your child about this in advance. Let him know what your new plan will be. It might sound something like this: "Mommy doesn't like to yell and get mad. So when I get upset I'm going to put my hands up like this and I am going to say 'STOP!' This means that I am getting mad and I need to stop talking and calm down." Demonstrate what you will do with your hands as you say this. There are two advantages to explaining your plan in advance. First, your child will know what to expect and why you're doing it, so you won't catch him off guard. Second, it shows him a productive way to handle his own anger.

Releasing Your Anger—but Not at Your Child

What if you are so angry at your child that you are ready to strike him and you cannot find the restraint to use your STOP gesture? In that case, channel your physical reaction into a burst of applause. Granted, it won't be happy applause. When you feel

Mother-Speak

"We use a silent scream in our house to release anger. It is just like a full-throated regular scream with screwed-up face and eyes, wide-open mouth, clenched fists, and a tight and vibrating body—just without the sound. I've taught my daughters how to use it when they get angry. After a particularly busy and frustrating morning, my daughter Willow suggested that I use one as I grumbled at the traffic. It was fabulous. Although I think the other drivers might've thought I was crazy, it saved me from losing my temper!"

—Jane, mother to Isla, age 5, and Willow, age 4

yourself about to strike, clap your hands. Clap them hard and fast, while you express your feelings of anger. Try it now. Pretend you're angry, clap your hands, and tell your imaginary child how you feel. ("OH! I am so angry right now!!") You'll find that in addition to releasing your pent-up anger, clapping will send a very clear message to your child.

When to STOP

This anger management technique of acknowledging anger and stopping yourself can be used for all problems. It can be effective with everything from minor irritations that bring irrational anger to major problems that require a clear head to solve. The time frame on this step can be anywhere from a few minutes to a day or more, depending on how upset you are and how big the problem is that you must deal with—and how quickly your must address the issue with a solution.

To recap, once you sense that you are losing control use your STOP gesture and words to halt the evolution of anger.

Step 2: Space

Now that you've stopped, you need to step away from your child. When you are angry, the *last* thing you need to do is stay engaged in the situation that is making you mad—all that does is escalate your anger. Suppose your child is whining and fussing and it has driven you to anger. You call out "STOP" but then you stay in the room while she continues to whine and fuss. You will likely just get worked right back up to anger again. This is the time to put some space between you and your child.

> **Mother-Speak**
> "It's a good idea to speak to your children before an angry outburst occurs and let them know what to expect so they aren't shocked by your departure. 'When Mommy gets angry, Mommy may need to go to her room to cool down. What could you do while you're waiting for Mommy to cool down? Mommy really wants to be calm and not yell.'"
> —**Kim, mother to Lily, age 8, and Benny, age 3**

Creating this space might involve putting a baby into the crib, placing a toddler in a safe place for a time-out (or even putting her in front of the TV), or turning your back on a whining child. If your child doesn't willingly separate from you, it's not the time to get into a shouting match over making her go—just put yourself in the bedroom or bathroom for your own time-out. If you cannot leave the room, then cross your arms, shut your eyes, and stand still. Put on your music headset and create your own private space right there in the middle of the room.

Putting space between you and your child accomplishes a number of things. First, it communicates your dissatisfaction to your child—it lets her know that you are too upset to continue. It prevents the episode from getting out of control. It allows you to calm yourself down so that you will have the presence of mind to solve the problem that is upsetting you. One other advantage to using this technique—it teaches your child an important anger management skill. You are setting a good example of how to walk away instead of proceeding with angry or hurtful words and actions.

If you need to stop a dangerous situation, or if you need to separate children who are fighting, do so before walking away, but do it without discussion—hold your thoughts for later.

Remember that almost every parenting problem can wait. It doesn't require an immediate resolution. Don't worry—it will still be there when you are ready to face it. *(Darn.)*

It is critically important that at this point you do *not* try to deal with the situation that is making you angry. You cannot solve a problem in a fit of anger; it will likely just escalate the situation or create a new layer of problems to deal with. You are going to step away from your child so that you can calm and collect yourself and, very likely, allow your child to calm down a bit, too.

Alternate Step 2: Squeeze
If you STOP and find that your control is now in place, you don't have to go on to creating space. Instead, change that to *squeeze*—embrace your child in a big bear hug. Do not talk. Just hug. And allow your anger to evaporate in the embrace.

Take a deep breath and repeat a calming mantra. "She's just a child." "I can handle this." "This too shall pass." Take a minute to look at your child and try to find the love that is hidden there. Remind yourself that she won't be little for long, and someday—trust me—you will miss this period of time.

The hug does *not* mean that you have accepted the misbehavior—you'll still have to deal with that. However, it does tell your child that you love her and will work through any problems. Think about it from the reverse perspective. Let's say that you are in charge of paying the credit card bill. One month you put the envelope in a drawer and forget to pay it. Your spouse is at a business lunch and attempts to pay the bill, but the card is denied. Having no cash, your spouse must ask the other person to pay the bill. Once home, your spouse confronts you with the problem and is very angry, of course. You feel sick about it. In the middle of it all, your spouse gives you a big hug. You know you're not off the hook, but you do know that you are loved in spite of your mistake.

At any point in the six-step sequence you can switch to a squeeze if you find yourself in control and longing to just hug your child. Remember that doing so doesn't mean you condone the bad behavior—it just means you love your child.

Mother-Speak

"I used the squeeze method the other day. My little girl, Derryn, had her tonsils taken out and was miserable. I guess my son, Wade, was feeling jealous of all the attention she was getting, so he was being very difficult. Instead of the usual moan, I picked him up and put him on my lap and gave him a big hug. I reflected to him how he must be feeling with his sister not well and being a bit grumpy, and the fact that all the adults were very concerned about her. I also mentioned that he might be feeling a bit left out and also sad that his sister couldn't play with him. Well, he looked at me and nodded. I gave him another hug and off he went to play. It was quite amazing and also so gratifying to have 'connected' with him on a level he understood rather than create distance between us by just groaning at him. This really worked for us, and I will try to use it more often."

—Heidi, mother to Wade, age 4, and Derryn, age 2

Step 3: Soothe

Once you have stopped your angry flow and separated yourself from your child, take some time to calm and collect yourself.

Begin by controlling your internal, physical responses to anger. Likely your heart rate is increased, your breathing is rapid, your face is flushed, or your voice is raised. You may also be experiencing any number of other indicators discussed previously. No matter what your physical symptoms are, the first step to inner control is to breathe deeply.

Breathing deeply allows your body to fill with oxygen. This will stop the adrenaline rush that floods your body when you are angry. This extra oxygen flow will relax your body, calm your breathing, slow your heart rate, and allow your brain to resume rational thought.

As you breathe deeply, you may want to close your eyes (or look at something that usually pleases you, such as a special photograph, your garden, or the sky) and take a number of slow, even, deep breaths. Put your hand on your stomach and carry the air down until you feel your stomach rise.

For a few minutes do not think about the situation that is upsetting you. Remember, it will wait. It may take some distraction to pull your thoughts away from the situation. Try counting, reciting a poem, or repeating a calming word or phrase, such as "Relax, it's okay," "This too shall pass," or "God, please help me."

Sometimes this breathing/relaxing isn't enough, and you'll find your mind continuing to return to your angry thoughts and winding you right back up again. If this happens, do something different for a time—watch TV, read, listen to music, run on your treadmill, or call a friend (but don't talk about the problem just yet).

There may be other ways that you can soothe and calm yourself. Think about the things you enjoy that most relax you. You may find that yoga, meditation, knitting, singing, or praying works for you. If another adult is able to tend to your children, you might find a brisk walk or jog can help clear your head.

Allow yourself the time for the tension to leave your body and to let the angry feelings subside. At this time you can regain your composure and will begin to think more clearly. Only then are you ready to move forward and begin to solve the problem.

Step 4: See

In order to solve the problem, you must see what is really happening. In order to fix anything you need to define the problem. But first you must figure out what went wrong. At the time of your anger, your view of the situation was skewed and your emotions stood in the way of truly seeing what was happening. Now that

Isabella, age 2½

you've calmed down, try to see what really happened. You can rewind the scene in your head and figure out what your child was doing (or not doing), what you wanted him to do instead, and why it upset you so much.

A good way to analyze what happened is to imagine that it happened to someone else—your sister, your brother, or a friend. Or, imagine that the scene took place on television and you are called in as the "expert" to analyze what went wrong. Looking at the situation as an outsider might help you see the truth. You might more clearly understand where your anger came from, or you may see that your reaction was way out of proportion—you were about to smack your daughter because she wouldn't eat her green beans!

As you "see" what happened, try to focus on the issue at hand. Don't review every other misbehavior that has ever happened in your home, except if it is directly related to this particular case. In other words, thinking about the fact that your non-green-bean-eating daughter hasn't put away her toys or fed the dog can confuse the issue, except to acknowledge that her pattern of not listening to you may be the real problem. The green beans were just the straw that broke the camel's back.

As part of the seeing process, try to adjust any unreasonable or unrealistic expectations that you have. Remember that the further our expectations are from reality, the more chance that our anger will escalate. So you might even grab a book on child development and check to see if this behavior is normal or typical.

Once you see the situation from a more objective point of view, then you can get a better grip on what's happening and begin to make some rational decisions—before confronting your child. Making this effort to view the situation dispassionately can help you clarify your long-term discipline and parenting objectives, rather than giving in to the tunnel vision of the short-term clash of wills.

Step 5: Specify

Now it's time to define the *exact* problem. After you have seen the situation more clearly, it is time to precisely define the problem in exact words. See if you can come up with a description of the problem in one or two sentences. Put it in clear, plain words that exactly state the real issue that sparked your anger.

It is rare that one isolated action sets off an angry outburst. It certainly isn't good behavior that sets off an angry exchange. Even if your anger originates with one of the mistaken beliefs described in Part 1 or if you lost control because you have a short fuse due to stress, pain, or a bad mood, it is still most likely that the issue that set you off really is misbehavior—typically misbehavior that you deal with repeatedly. You likely don't explode when your child is quietly and happily drawing at the kitchen table. In other words, even if your angry response is inappropriate, it probably has roots in a valid problem.

Try to specify your exact dilemma. Begin with "The problem is . . ." exercise. Here are a few examples:

The problem is . . . she has temper tantrums in public.

The problem is . . . he backtalks and sasses me.

The problem is . . . she makes a mess and won't clean up.

The problem is . . . when I tell him to do something he ignores my request.

The problem is . . . they won't share and they fight over toys.

The problem is . . . she's tired and cranky but won't take a nap.

When the Problem Isn't About Your Child

What if you analyze the situation and discover (to your surprise) that the real problem wasn't something your child did but your inappropriate loss of temper? What if you realize that your angry emotions propelled you to blow the situation way out of proportion? What if you are able to honestly evaluate what happened and discover that this explosion wasn't about your child at all? Or perhaps, it was somewhat about your child but mainly about *you*. This is one of the most difficult situations for a parent to face.

The best solution is to apologize, but this isn't always easy. This is often a very complex suggestion, for a number of reasons. Often, your child did misbehave and her action triggered your anger. So even though your response was inappropriate, the child's behavior was inappropriate as well. In addition, parents often feel that by apologizing for their anger they are relieving the child of any responsibility for her part in the event. And, if you have made loud and firm statements in your angry tirade, it feels foolish to go back and eat your words. So sometimes you continue to defend your angry words and actions, even though you were wrong *and* you know you were wrong.

As hard as it may be, there are times when the best thing you can do is admit to yourself that you were wrong and apologize to your child for losing your temper. Apologizing at the right time can teach your child very important lessons about life. It shows her that no one is exempt from making mistakes. It shows her that apologizing is a right thing to do.

Father-Speak

"I am never too old to apologize or too proud to ask my children for forgiveness."

—Brian, father to Michael, age 9; Nathan, age 6; and Karah, age 1

If your child was also wrong, you can explain that although your response was inappropriate, her behavior was as well. Avoid turning this into a lecture, and don't imply that your child is responsible for your actions. Instead, use this as a life lesson in humility. Perhaps your apology can be a model for your child's own apology.

Keep in mind that your apologies to your child should be brief and few. If you find that you are in the position to apologize too often to your child, then perhaps you should consider talking to a family counselor for advice on how to better control your angry outbursts.

Let's now move on to the last of our six steps to staying calm. Once you have clearly identified the cause of your anger and specified the exact problem, you then can move to solving the problem.

Step 6: Solve

Now . . . it's time to solve the problem and move forward with action. By this point you will be calm and composed and you will have clearly identified what went wrong. It is time to decide how best to apply your parenting skills to solve the dilemma. Of course, it helps if you actually have good parenting skills to apply—that's what the rest of this book is about!

Once you've stated the problem, you can then consider options for solving it. You may want to jot down several possible options on paper or talk about options with another adult. This may also be a good time to read through a few of your favorite parenting books and check the indexes for your problem topic. You could also talk it over with another adult or in an online parenting chat group or posting board. There's no reason for you to make decisions in a vacuum. I guarantee that the problem you are dealing with is a common one and there are lots of sources for solutions.

Follow Through

Once you've taken these six steps you will be very ready to return to your child to address the situation that brought about your anger. You'll be calm and in control, and you'll have a plan. All that's left is to follow through on what you've set out to do.

Keep in mind that it takes much more than a one-time reading of this information to change your actions. It may take several readings, plus lots of practice, before you find that you are handling your anger in a consistently productive way. You are changing not only what you do, but what your child does. And you are often changing a pattern that has been in place for many months, or even years.

Mother-Speak

"My husband was away on business last night so it was up to me to get both children to sleep. I read Wade a story and then gave him a new Winnie the Pooh book with CD to listen to while I tended to Derryn. I got the CD going in his room and tucked him in with it, promising to be back as soon as Derryn was asleep. I joined him when Derryn was sleeping and read and listened to one of the stories with him.

"Once it was over, I said good night and switched the CD off. That's when the upset began. He didn't want to go to sleep, and he was desperate to listen to one more story. I said, 'No, it's time to sleep.' I tucked him in and said good night. He cried and got off his bed and followed me to the kitchen. I picked him up and put him back in his bed. Then he kicked and fussed and wailed about wanting another story. After ten minutes of this I felt myself getting angry.

I had a million things I needed to do before getting to bed myself, and my patience was wearing thin.

"I remembered your anger steps, so I put my hand up, palm out, and said, 'Stop. Just stop this now. I'm getting angry.' I stepped away from him for a minute, took a deep breath, and calmed down. Then I went back and took him in my arms and gave him a big hug, saying, 'I know you're upset because you want to listen to more stories. What I'd like to hear you say is 'Thank you, Mommy, for my new book and CD and for letting me listen to the stories. I'm looking forward to tomorrow night when I can listen to another one.' He hugged me back, and after a minute he said, 'Thank you, Mommy, for my new book. Can I listen to it again tomorrow?' I gave him a squeeze and told him he could. He then went peacefully to sleep.

"I felt so good that the meltdown had not turned ugly. I hope that I can use your method more and more before I get too emotionally upset and the opportunity is lost. It was very, very rewarding."

—**Heidi, mother to Wade, age 4, and Derryn, age 2**

Be kind to yourself. Anger is a difficult emotion to control. Even when you've mastered all the skills in this book, there will still be times when anger gets the best of you. You'll lose control with your child, and then you'll berate yourself for not remembering to use the steps to staying calm. But, try to forgive yourself as you forgive your child. If you can use what you learn to eliminate even half of the anger episodes in your life, you will be far ahead of many, many parents.

Sage, age 3½

Change takes time. Also, don't underestimate the fact that these ideas are best used with the ideas from Parts 1 and 2 of this book. If you don't change your approach to discipline, then the source of your anger will still pop up again and again.

On page 188 you'll find a list of the Six Steps to Staying Calm. Copy and post it in a visible place in your home. At first you'll rely on this reminder to help you through the steps. Practice this sequence whenever you are irritable or tense. Eventually, you may begin to use the steps automatically whenever anger takes hold. And that will be a day worth celebrating!

Reducing Anger-Producing Situations

This book is about developing good discipline practices that will, in turn, reduce the types of misbehaviors that tend to make you angry. Here are a few quick tips to get you thinking about how you can stop those situations that make you mad—before they even happen.

- Learn and practice good parenting skills.
- Take a bit of nonparenting personal time for yourself every day.
- Keep a written schedule or calendar of your responsibilities to prevent haphazard chaos.
- Post clear and understandable family rules.
- Offer your children choices instead of making demands, whenever possible.
- Make your requests brief and clear.
- Express yourself using "I" sentences; avoid "you" statements that can create conflict.
- Get to eye level when talking to your child (don't shout from two rooms away).
- Pick your battles—not every issue is worth fighting over.
- Increase your support system—join a parent club, visit an online parenting chat site, or make friends with the parents of your children's playmates.

Do You Need
More Help?

There are times when people are taught anger management skills but the information doesn't match their personality, doesn't address an underlying reason for anger, or isn't enough to help them to control their emotions. If the six steps to staying calm don't help you stay calm, then answer these questions with a yes or no.

- Have you read and studied this chapter and posted the review page, but your anger still gets the better of you?
- Do you lose your temper over both big and small issues?
- Are your angry episodes frequent and/or intense?
- Do your angry feelings last for a long time after the situation that caused them?
- When you are angry do you hit, slam, throw, or break things or hurt people?
- Do you find that your spouse or children are becoming afraid of you?
- Are you afraid of yourself when you get mad?
- Is your anger worse now than it used to be?

If you answered yes to any of these questions, you may have difficulty handling anger and require more assistance than this book can offer. There are many places where you can get caring, supportive help for learning how to control your anger. You may want to explore several options, since there are various approaches used for anger management. Possible options for getting the help that you need, either through classes, group workshops, or individual counseling, include a

- local hospital
- school counselor
- priest, minister, or other religious leader
- family doctor
- counselor, therapist, psychologist, or other mental health professional

Don't be afraid to ask for help. Your family will be so much better off if you do, and you will be proud that you took such positive action. Your family is worth it.

Reminder Page
Six Steps to Staying Calm

Step 1: Stop
Identify your angry feelings.
Raise your hands to signal STOP. Stop talking.

Step 2: Space
Move away from your child or move your child away from
you.
Alternate choice if calm: **Squeeze**—give your child a big hug.

Step 3: Soothe
Calm yourself.
Take a deep breath, repeat a relaxing phrase, pray, or practice
yoga.
Read, listen to music, or exercise.

Step 4: See
Replay what happened in your mind's eye.
Analyze the situation objectively.

Step 5: Specify
Define the *exact* problem ("The problem is . . .").

Step 6: Solve
Decide which parenting skills to use.
Create several possible solutions.
Follow through.

Part 4

Specific Solutions for
Everyday Problems

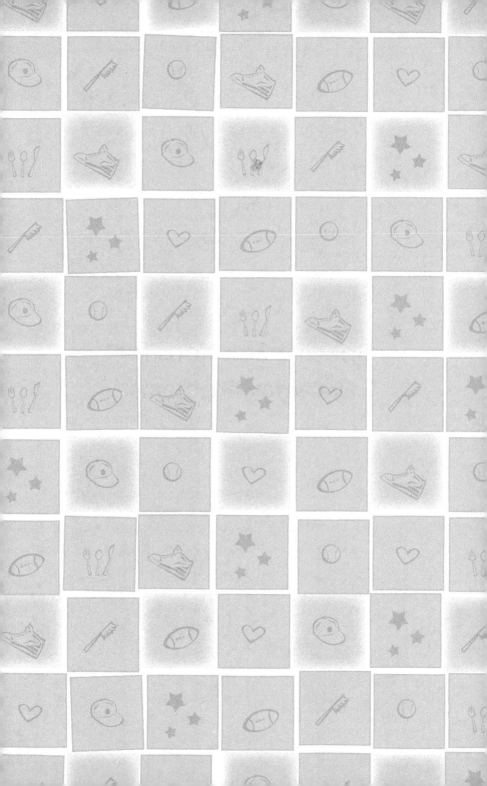

Applying No-Cry Parenting Skills to Everyday Problems

U ntil now, we've covered basic parenting skills. You can use these skills to solve nearly any behavior issue you face. Sometimes, though, there's so much information rolling around in your head that it's hard to sift through all the skills you've learned and come up with a specific solution at a given moment. The chapters that follow will provide some quick tips for the most common discipline problems parents face during the early childhood years.

It is critical to keep in mind that your child's age and level of understanding will affect the way you'll respond in any given situation. How you'll approach a two-year-old who has a tantrum is very different than how you will approach a six-year-old having a tantrum—even if both children are having tantrums because they are tired, hungry, and rebelling after you said no potato chips. Younger children will require much more teaching and direction than older ones who have already had years of lessons from you. In addition, you'll have to honestly assess how *you* have responded to your child in the past, as the history between you will affect both of your reactions today. You can't abruptly change your way of interacting with your child and expect him to modify his responses to suit your new goals.

All children are unique. There isn't one perfect solution that works for every single child. Even siblings can be very different from one another. I have four children who are as alike as apples, oranges, brownies, and chewing gum. It often amazes me that these four children were birthed by the same parents and raised in the same home. They are very distinctive individuals, and they have very different strengths and personality traits. They each require very different things from me, yet other things from their dad. When parents expect all children to act exactly the same, or if they expect the same child to respond precisely the same way in every situation (which they don't!), they set themselves up for frustration. That's why I think that it's important for us to have a wide repertoire of parenting skills so we can modify what we do to make our discipline plan work best for each child in our family, and in each different situation.

The best advice I can give you is to be flexible and ambidextrous! As each situation arises, apply what you learn to each of your children in the unique and special way that is best for them. Then take pleasure in the variety and spice that they give to your life.

Each of the following topics could easily fill an entire book, and there are several hundred additional topics that could be added to this list. So, what you'll find in the following pages are a handful of the most common discipline-related problems that occur during early childhood, along with a variety of solutions for each issue. The solutions all have a common denominator: respect—for both child and parent. In addition, these solutions can help you to avoid anger and tears (both your child's and yours). All the options will help you guide your child to become a thoughtful person with healthy self-discipline and self-esteem. Yet the options are varied, allowing you to customize your response to best suit both you and

Mother-Speak

"The list of topics in this section sounds like my three-year-old daughter's daily 'to-do' list!"

—Patti, mother to Maddison, age 3, and Mason, age 1

your individual child, leading you toward the best solution in each situation.

The combination of solutions for each problem that follows is diverse. I don't mean for you to follow every single suggestion as if it were a road map. These ideas are meant to act as a starting point for you to develop your own customized solution. With this in mind, the following chapters provide you with a number of practical solutions for solving each type of parenting problem.

When you are struggling with a behavior issue, look up that particular topic and any other similar topics, as you might pick up pointers in various places. Look over the ideas, combine them with the other skills you've learned throughout this book, and customize them to create several options that suit your family. Review your options, and consider your child's personality, your parenting style, and your family goals. Then put your decision into action. If your original plan doesn't bring success, try another option, and, on occasion, even a third option, until you feel good about how things are going. Remember: This too shall pass. Relax, take a deep breath, and remember to hug your child.

Baby Talk

My preschooler has gotten in the habit of talking in a baby voice. When she was a baby, that kind of talk was adorable. Now that she's not, it's extremely annoying.

Think About It

This is a normal stage of behavior. Many preschoolers think that talking like a baby makes them sound more cute and lovable. It's one of those phases that will pass on its own but can be frustrating in the meantime when you want your child to "act her age." You can give nature a nudge and move your child past the baby-talk stage more quickly by using some of the following suggestions.

What to Do

- **Give more attention.** Children sometimes use baby talk to hold on to babyhood as they take a developmental step forward. It's a way for them to feel safely rooted in the familiar cared-for environment they are used to—but that they know they must leave behind. Acknowledge this as a real need, and give your child a bit more loving attention. A few extra hugs or a chance to sit on your lap or hold your hand may build her sense of security and give her the courage she needs to grow forward.

- **Express your feelings.** Let your child know how much the baby talk bothers you. Ask for her help in changing the behavior.

"The baby talk really bothers me, and I love your big-girl voice very much. Will you please use your regular voice for me?"

- **Fail to understand her.** When she says, "Me wanna gas of mik." Look at her with a very confused look on your face and say, "I can't understand. What do you want?" This should be easy, since you probably don't fully understand her anyway. Don't respond to her request until she uses her normal voice.

- **Be silly.** Intentionally interpret her baby-talk request into something ridiculous, like "Did you say you want some lima beans and liver?"

- **Give your child more responsibilities.** Help her to see that she is growing up, and encourage her with praise. Choose fun tasks for her, such as helping to prepare the salad for dinner, feeding the cat, or sweeping the floor. Often, when a child begins to see herself as a big kid, the baby talk will disappear.

What Not to Do

- **Don't assume she's doing this to annoy you.** This reversion to baby behavior isn't intended to irritate you, because it's not about you at all. Sometimes it's a sign that your child is sorting through her feelings about growing up and leaving her babyhood behind.

- **Don't mimic or mock her baby talk.** Your child may not be fully aware of what she is doing or how often, so don't call it to her attention in an angry or sarcastic manner.

Backtalk

....

See also: Bossiness; Hitting a Parent; Swearing, Bad Language, and Bathroom Jokes

I always thought backtalk was something older kids did, but my four-year-old is proving me wrong.

Think About It

The first time a child talks back to a parent, it is usually just an honest emotion being expressed, typically indicating he doesn't like something. The problem is not the child's opinion—which he is entitled to—the real problem is the way that opinion is voiced. If the parent doesn't correct the way the child is communicating—then and there—the pattern will continue and become worse over time because the child will assume that this is an acceptable way to express his feelings.

What to Do

- **Identify it.** When your child talks back to you, immediately call attention to it. Look your child in the eye and, in a serious voice, firmly say something like, "That is backtalk and not a proper way to tell me what you think." Then, since you want to teach good manners, use your good manners as you request, "Please don't talk to Mommy that way."
- **Teach.** Your child is talking back to you because he disagrees with you. His disagreement is not the problem; his manner of deal-

196

Jobe, age 2

ing with it is the problem. Teach him how to politely and respectfully voice his opinion by demonstrating how to communicate
politely. "What I want to hear you say is, 'Mommy, can I please
play a little longer?' That's using your good manners."

• **Watch for bad influences.** Keep your eye on your child's
friends and older siblings. Pay attention to TV programs that are
on when your child is in the room. Children imitate other people,
which is how they learn. What goes in children's ears often comes
out their mouths.

• **Be consistent.** This is a situation that will come up from time
to time during childhood, and it can be curbed with calm guidance. The key is to be unswerving in your dedication to address
every single episode of backtalk.

What Not to Do

- **Don't empower it.** Whenever your child talks back, don't let it turn into a two-way argument between equals. The issue is not the subject that caused the backtalk, anyway. It is the backtalk itself that needs to be addressed.

- **Don't ignore it.** You must be consistent in your response to backtalk. If you selectively ignore it, depending on how it happens or when it happens, then you can count on having to deal with more and more sass over time.

- **Don't shout or slap.** A child who erupts with a biting, sarcastic remark can bring out the worst in parents, who feel shockingly disrespected and unloved. Responding with knee-jerk anger may startle your child into silence, but it won't solve the problem.

Bath, Not Behaving In

See also: Bath, Not Wanting One;
Bath, Won't Get Out

> Bath time at our house is a disaster. My daughter
> splashes, throws toys, and sprays the entire bathroom
> with water. Washing up doesn't happen without a
> big fuss.

Think About It

For many children, the tub is a grand private swimming pool and washing up is last on their list of priorities. They're not being naughty—they are just having fun!

What to Do

- **Have a specific list of bathtub rules.** Children can't guess what you expect of them in every situation. It helps to clearly express your expectations. State your rules in a way that lets your child know exactly what you *want*, rather than what you *don't want*. As an example, instead of saying, "No splashing," a better rule is "Keep all water in the tub" or "Keep the bath rug dry."
- **Put only a few inches of water in the tub.** Tell your child that when she shows you that she has learned how to keep the water in the bathtub, you'll increase the amount of water you put in the next time.

- **Allow a shower instead.** If your child is six or older, have her take a shower instead of a bath.
- **Join 'em.** If you have a younger child and you're comfortable with family nudity (or with bathing in a swimsuit), you can sometimes get in the tub with her and have a good time splashing together.
- **Relax, it's just water.** It may help if you budget extra time for a bath and put up a clear shower curtain and close it while your child splashes and plays. That way you can still see in the tub, but the water stays contained. Bring a chair and a book into the bathroom and enjoy a few minutes of relaxation. Water play is free and lots of fun, so if you can make it work for you, bath time can be a great play experience for your child.

What Not to Do

- **Don't let this routine continue.** Children are creatures of habit, and your daughter's bath play is a fun routine for her. In order to change things you'll need to revamp your entire bath time routine.
- **Don't make bath time playtime.** If toys and wild play are the problem, then don't put any toys in the tub for a while. Get your child into the tub, washed up, and out of the tub quickly. Over time, as bath time gets under control, provide a couple of toys and see how it goes.
- **Don't complain without action.** If every time your child wrecks havoc in the tub the only consequence is hearing you complain about it, then she'll have no reason or motivation to change.

Bath, Not Wanting One

....

See also: Bath, Not Behaving In; Bath, Won't Get Out

> My child never wants to take a bath. She doesn't
> cooperate at all, and it becomes a battle.

Think About It

Take a minute to stop and think about *why* your child doesn't want to take a bath. Is it because she's having too much fun doing other things and doesn't want to stop? Is it because bath time usually includes a battle of wills? Is it because she always gets soap in her eyes? Or is it because it signals the beginning of the bedtime routine? Once you figure out the real reason, you can take steps to move past the problem.

What to Do

- **Make it fun.** Allow your child to use bubble bath or children's bath foam to make it more fun. Buy a few fun bath toys or use plastic kitchen products for play. Allow your child to play for a while before washing up.
- **Control the suds.** If your child fears getting soap in her eyes when you wash her hair, let her wear swimming goggles or a plastic sun visor while you do the washing.
- **Be very consistent.** Have a bath every day or every other day at exactly the same time *and* in the same way. Specific routines can overcome resistance after they've become regular occurrences.

• **Give a forewarning.** Let your child know ahead of time that bath time is nearing. Give a few warnings. "Bath time in ten minutes." Then, "Bath time in five minutes." Your child will respond better with warnings than if you just drop the bomb in the middle of her fun activity.

• **Change your routine.** Bath time is often done at bedtime when a child and the parent are tired and grumpy. In addition, if your child knows that bedtime follows a bath she may want to put off the entire sequence. Instead, let your child bathe first thing in the morning when everyone is fresh and energetic.

What Not to Do

• **Don't lecture about the importance of personal hygiene.** Hygiene isn't the reason your child avoids the bath—she isn't even thinking about that aspect of bathing. It's the time that it takes and the process involved that she objects to.

• **Don't wheel and deal.** Parents inadvertently get into the practice of bargaining with their children. "If you get in the bath right now, then I'll let you have bubbles." Bribes are the wrong approach to gaining cooperation, taking power away from the parent and giving it to the child. Bribes are different from rewards or encouragement. Bubbles offered to a child up front, to make the bath more fun, are fine. Bubbles offered to stop a tantrum could be seen as a reward for misbehavior or as incentive for future tantrums.

Bath, Won't Get Out

....

See also: Bath, Not Behaving In; Bath, Not Wanting One; Dawdling

My child doesn't listen to me when I say it's time to get out of the tub.

Think About It

Your child probably doesn't want to get *in* the tub either! You might notice that your child doesn't adjust quickly to any kind of change. Often, the problem occurs when he's doing something fun (splashing in the tub) and has to stop and do something that's not so fun (get dressed and ready for bed). A little motivation goes a long way in helping this child adjust to changes.

What to Do

- **Use a timer.** Set it for a predetermined amount of bath time. Give a five-minute warning and then a three-minute warning before the timer goes off. Announce that when the timer rings your child will need to get out of the tub. At the timer's ding, be pleasant about getting him out of the tub. Once he's used to this routine he'll go along with it.
- **Offer a choice.** Giving children choices moves them in your direction because they have a say in what's happening and are more willing to cooperate. When it's time to get out, stand by the edge of the tub, hold out a towel, and offer a choice, such as, "Do

you want to dry your hair by yourself, or do you want me to help you?"

• **Use the "when/then" technique.** Give your child a reason to get out of the tub. Promise something fun after the bath is done. "When you are out of the tub and dressed, then we'll have some hot cocoa and read a book."

• **Get silly!** Make a game out of the process. Sing a song, or hold the towel like a puppet and make it talk to your child.

• **Mean what you say.** Don't tell your child it's time to get out of the tub until you really mean it's time to get out of the tub. Repeating yourself five or six times until you mean business is only setting yourself up for a struggle the next time and the next time and the next.

What Not to Do

• **Don't spring it on him.** If your child is having a grand time in the bath, don't suddenly whisk him out without prior warning.

• **Don't dawdle or waiver.** Multiple requests, nagging, and pleading for compliance inform your child that listening to you is optional and that he can get out of the bath when he's ready.

• **Don't yell, threaten, or pull the plug.** Getting angry will only lead to your child's tears and an unpleasant end to the day for both of you. And drastic solutions like draining the tub, dragging a child out of the bath, or avoiding baths entirely are all disrespectful to both child and parent.

Biting, Child to Adult

See also: Biting Other Children; Hitting a Parent

> When I was getting my son dressed this morning, he got upset over my choice of T-shirt for him. As I was putting it over his head, he bit my arm. I was so startled by this that I nearly cried!

Think About It

It's natural to be shocked or hurt by your child's actions, but rest assured that your little one didn't intend to injure you—he just couldn't find the right words or actions to get his point across. So, a quick bite seemed like the right solution at the time. It helps when you understand that this behavior is normal and that it's not intentional misconduct. Nonetheless, it is something you'll want to put a halt to immediately. This is an opportunity to teach him an important lesson in social skills.

What to Do

- **Respond humanly.** Go with your natural response. Say, "Ouch! That hurts!" Often, your startled response will send a message to your child that what just happened wasn't a good thing. He may even start to cry, which indicates his understanding that he hurt you. You can then encourage him to apologize and ask him to kiss the place where he bit, if this is how you make his boo-boos feel better. He will soon make the connection.

- **Watch for early signs of frustration.** When you see that your child is unhappy, angry, or frustrated, help him to express his feelings with words. You may need to even start him out by giving him the specific words he needs, such as, "I can see that you don't want to wear this shirt. You can say to me, 'Mommy, I don't want this shirt.'"

- **Respond firmly.** Use a no-nonsense voice and tell your child, "Stop! No biting. It hurts." Move away from him for a few minutes so that he understands that his actions don't bring him positive attention.

- **Avoid biting him in play.** Children are so incredibly sweet that parents sometimes nibble their little fingers, toes, or bellies. Parents sometimes play biting games with young children. "See if you can put your finger in my mouth without it chomping shut." Doing these things, though, might confuse your child, who may have a hard time understanding when a bite is okay and when it's not. So, if you have a child who has taken a bite out of you or a playmate, it's best if you avoid playful biting.

What Not to Do

- **Don't bite your child back.** You don't have to demonstrate to make your point. This might reinforce his idea that biting is a feasible solution to a problem. It certainly will create confusion about what you are trying to teach.

- **Don't respond in a distressed, angry, or pleading way.** If you overreact or accuse your child of intentionally hurting you, then you might frighten him and prevent him from learning a valuable lesson from the experience.

- **Don't worry.** There's nothing "wrong" with your child; he isn't bad. He's reacting in a very normal way for his stage of development.

Biting Other Children

See also: Biting, Child to Adult; Hitting, Kicking, and Hair Pulling; Sibling Fights

Today at the park my son bit my friend's daughter on the arm! I'm horrified!

Think About It

Biting a playmate is a common occurrence among young children since they don't always have the words to describe their emotions. They don't quite know how to control their feelings, and they don't have any concept of hurting another person. When a child bites a friend, it most likely isn't an act of aggression. It is simply an immature way of trying to get a point across, experimentation with cause and effect, or playfulness gone awry.

What to Do

• **Watch and intercept.** As you become familiar with your child's emotional actions, you may be able to stop a bite before it even occurs. If you see that your child is getting frustrated or angry—perhaps in the middle of a tussle about a toy—step in and redirect her attention to something else.

• **Teach.** Immediately after your child bites another child, look her in the eye and tell her in one or two short sentences what you want her to know and how she can make amends. "Biting hurts.

Amelia, age 2

We don't bite. Please say you're sorry and ask Emmy if she'd like a hug. That might make her feel better."

• **Give your child lessons on how she should handle her frustrations.** Your child is going to get upset with a playmate, so teach her some ways to handle her feelings. Tell her what she should say or do. "If you want a toy, you can ask nicely for it or come to Mommy for help."

• **Avoid playful biting.** Nibbling your little one's toes or playfully nipping her fingers sends a mixed message to your child. A child won't understand when biting another person is okay and when it's not, nor is she able to judge the pressure she's putting into the bite. As she gets a little older, she will start to understand that some things can be done carefully and gently in play but not in anger. This takes more maturity to understand—more than you can expect your child to have at her young age.

- **Give more attention to the injured child.** Typically, we put all our energy into correcting the biter's actions and we don't give the child who was bitten much consolation. The little victim is left sitting alone, crying. Soothing the child who was hurt can show your child that her actions caused another child fear or pain. You can even encourage your child to help soothe her friend with a pat on the back or a hug.

- **Handle the repeat offender.** If you've gone through the previous steps and your child bites again, you can respond with more intensity. If you catch her in the act, immediately go to her. Get down to her level, look her in the eye, and firmly announce, "No biting. Take a time-out." Direct her to a chair and have her sit for a few minutes. It won't take long for your message to sink in.

- **React even when you don't see it.** If you miss the action but are told about it later, have a talk with your child about what happened. Limit yourself to a few brief, specific comments, remembering that a lengthy lecture is almost never effective. Reading children's books together on the topic, role-playing, and demonstrating appropriate actions can all help your child learn how to respond to her own emotions in socially appropriate ways.

- **Provide first aid.** Although the risk of injury from a child's bite is small, it's good to know what to do if a bite breaks through the skin. Reassure the child who was bitten. Wash your hands with soap and water and then the wound with soap and water. If the bite is bleeding, apply direct pressure with a clean, dry cloth. Cover the injury with a bandage.

What Not to Do

- **Don't respond emotionally.** When their child uses her teeth on another human being, parents' immediate response is often anger, followed by punishment. This is because we view the act from an adult perspective. However, if we can understand that a child's bite is most likely a responsive reflex, we can avoid responding in typical yet ineffective ways.

- **Don't bite your child back to "show her how it feels."** She isn't purposefully hurting her playmate. She likely doesn't understand that what she did is wrong, so by responding with the same action you may actually be reinforcing that this is an acceptable behavior, confusing her entirely.
- **Don't assume that your child is willfully misbehaving.** The ways that you'll treat these behaviors in an older child, who understands that biting is wrong, will be different than how you will approach this with young child.
- **Don't yell at your child.** This will do nothing more than scare her. Yelling won't teach her anything about what she's just done, nor does it teach her what she should have done instead.

Bossiness

See also: Backtalk

> My daughter is always telling her friends what to do.
> She decides what games to play and then makes the
> rules (which are ever changing). The other kids just go
> along with her now, but as she gets older,
> I'm sure they won't.

Think About It

Learning how to play with other children is a social skill that takes practice. If the other children go along with your daughter, then she's under the impression that all is well. You'll need to help her understand how to play politely. The good news is that a child who frequently takes the lead often develops into a strong leader. You'll just need to help her learn how to develop and refine her leadership skills.

What to Do

- **Discuss what you saw.** Stay calm and don't accuse, simply state what you saw. "I noticed that you kept taking the ball from Jeremy." Then ask what your child thinks of the situation. Direct the conversation with helpful questions. "How do you think your friend felt?" "Do you think you could have done something different?" "What should you do next time?"

- **Encourage your child to be a positive leader.** Teach the difference between a bossy statement and one that is assertive but respectful. She likely doesn't realize there is a subtle, but important, difference between the two. For example, "When you say, 'This is how we're going to play' it sounds bossy, but asking, 'How about if we do it this way?' is a polite way to suggest new rules."
- **Enroll your child in a team activity.** Have your child participate in a group activity such as Little League, scouting, a YMCA program, or a church youth group. Being part of a team or special group will your help child experience group play in a monitored situation and may help reduce her bossy behavior. Take the time to select a group with a polite and able leader. Look for a coach or director who is comfortable leading the group and who appears to enjoy spending time with young children.

Mother-Speak

"Lately I have found my son, Orrin, bossing around my husband and me and even our dogs. He makes demands, like 'Mom, come here now.' It's no wonder! This is exactly what he hears from us when we are asking something of him, so he has picked up on it. Now, when I hear him demand something like this, I tell him that he needs to ask nicely. He will then change his voice back to a nice voice and will say, 'Please, Mommy, will you come here?' Of course, the most important thing to learn from this is that we need to model for him the behavior that we want him to follow, so we are working on that, too."

—Tara, mother to Orrin, age 2, and Annalee, age 5 weeks

• **Determine if someone else is bossing your child around.** Is there an older sibling, babysitter, or friend who is bossing her? (Could it be *you*?) If you can modify this person's behavior to be more polite when requesting things of your child, that person can become a more positive role model.

• **Give the child responsibilities that she can be in charge of.** Let your child take care of a family pet or have responsibility for setting the table or watering a plant. Chores that encourage independence and give a child some control can fulfill the need your child has to be in charge of something.

• **Point out good behavior.** Watch your child and catch her doing something right—and then praise her for it.

What Not to Do

• **Don't make a public correction.** Reprimanding her in front of her friends will likely embarrass your daughter and her friends as well. Not only is this modeling poor manners for all of them, but it will prevent her from learning anything from the episode as she'll be hindered by her humiliation.

• **Don't stop having play dates.** Your child needs practice to develop better friendship skills. Over time, she'll learn how to socialize in more appropriate ways. You'll need to be more aware and involved until you see that things are running more smoothly.

• **Don't continually give in to your child's requests.** Make sure you aren't encouraging bossy behavior by always giving in to your child when the two of you are together. This is a pattern many parents get into when their children are babies, and they don't modify their responses to be more age appropriate over time.

- **Don't always play by her rules.** When you play with your child according to *her* rules—even when you don't want to play her way—you are promoting bossiness. Instead, encourage your child to learn how to play according to group rules, how to respect others' wishes, and how to compromise. Learning these things with a parent as the teacher is a comfortable, nonthreatening way to learn.

Car Problems

See also: Hitting, Kicking, and Hair Pulling; Other People's Undisciplined Children; Sibling Fights

We spend a lot of time in the car, and I get so frustrated over the same problems day after day. They don't want to sit in their booster seats, they fight with each other, and they whine and fuss at me.

Think About It

It's difficult for an active child to be strapped into a seat and required to be still for any length of time, but it is a necessary situation. Since you are in the car so often, you have a great opportunity to teach patience and to create and reinforce a routine that works for you. You'll just need to figure out what that routine is and then make it happen.

What to Do

- **Be firm about nonnegotiables.** Kids must be in car seats—it's the law. Tell them that a policeman could stop you, and you will all be in trouble if they aren't sitting properly in their seats. It also helps to explain that car seats keep them safe. But don't go into too much detail about car accidents, which could cause anxiety.
- **Create "car rules."** Write down your top rules and keep them in the car. Review them each time you get in the car. If necessary, plan a consequence for breaking the rules. For example, children

215

who break the rules get to clean the trash out of the car when you get home. Even a five-year-old can do this task. Remember to praise your children when you have an enjoyable ride and they follow the rules.

- **Keep them occupied.** Boredom can promote whining and fights. Keep books, travel games, car bingo cards, or music headsets in the car. It's also helpful to keep a few healthy snacks, such as dry cereal or pretzels, on hand. Children who are occupied or snacking are content and less likely to fuss or fight.

- **Take advantage of your captive audience.** Buy or borrow a selection of children's audio books and listen to them together. Talk about the story and use it as a launching pad for enriching discussions. Check your library or bookstore for a wonderful assortment of choices.

- **Give your children positive attention.** Keep the atmosphere in the car pleasant by using the time to talk to your children. Ask thought-provoking questions, recount the events of the week, or play guessing games. Your children will start looking forward to being in the car—and so will you.

- **Sing.** Turn on your favorite music or some children's sing-alongs. Have fun and sing!

What Not to Do

- **Don't add your own complaining and whining to the noise.** It doesn't help to voice your aggravation every time you take a drive. Complaining doesn't solve the problem; you need to create an active solution.

- **Don't pay more attention to the children than to your driving.** Distracted drivers are three times as likely to be involved in a car accident as more attentive drivers. Refereeing a backseat battle or tending to a whining child is very distracting. So keep

Mason, age 1, and Maddison, age 3

your eyes and your attention on the road. If your child's backseat tantrum upsets you, pull the car off the road. Park. Look your child in the eye and say, "When you stop I will drive." Turn around in your seat and wait. Read a book, look through your purse, do some stretches. If the behavior doesn't cease, repeat your statement, or, if possible, return home.

Dawdling

See also: Doesn't Come When Called

My son moves at an excruciatingly slow pace. When we need to get somewhere and I'm rushing about it is very frustrating to have to keep prodding him along.

Think About It

Children live according to a much slower clock than we adults do. They don't give a moment's thought to what they might be doing next. They prefer to enjoy each moment for what it is. They pause as they watch the cat sleep, examine the color patterns in the carpet, and ponder the reasons for having toes. If you think about it, it's a shame that we can't all live on "kid-time."

What to Do

• **Give specific step-by-step directions.** Make incremental requests that your child can easily follow. Give your child one or two tasks at a time, and when complete, assign the next. "Please put your puzzle in the box and go to the bathroom."

• **Make a list.** Write down the sequence of tasks to be completed, and give the list to your child with a pencil to cross things off as they're done.

• **Provide an incentive to finish.** Encourage your child to finish the task with a "when/then" statement, such as "When you get in the car, then you can have your crackers."

• **Analyze your own daily schedule.** Determine if you are trying to do too much. If you are, see if you can make some changes. Start focusing on the priorities in your life, eliminate some of the unnecessary time-wasters, and slow *yourself* down a little bit.

• **Check your child's nap and sleep schedules.** Children who aren't getting a proper amount of sleep will lack energy and tend to move slowly and dawdle.

What Not to Do

• **Don't rush your child by saying, "Come on!" or "Hurry up!"** These requests tend to frustrate children, and then they rush to the point of taking *extra* time to make up for the mistakes that happen when they move too fast.

• **Don't reinforce the pattern.** Children often dawdle out of habit. A parent will announce, "Time to go," and then be distracted by a phone call or a household task (so then it really *isn't* time to go). Children come to expect that you'll repeat yourself numerous times before they have to respond. Practice thinking before you speak, making a very specific request, and then following through.

• **Don't expect speed.** Allow a reasonable amount of time for your child to meet your request. Watch your child to learn his pace. Just because you are in a hurry doesn't mean your child will move any faster than his usual speed.

• **Don't miscommunicate.** Make clear, specific statements that don't leave room for misunderstanding. As an example, instead of the vague statement "Get ready to go," clarify by saying, "Right now, would you please put on your shoes and your coat and get in the car?"

Day Care or Preschool, Dropping Off and Picking Up

See also: Dawdling; Doesn't Come When Called

> My child dawdles and fusses when I drop her off at day care. You'd think she doesn't want to be there. I know she loves it because she repeats the behavior when I pick her up in the afternoon—she doesn't want to leave!

Think About It

Some children have a difficult time adjusting to changes. They like things to flow in a predictable way. Anything that upsets their current activity is cause for alarm. These children require a bit more thought to help them maneuver the changes they encounter during their day.

What to Do

• **Create very specific routines.** Consistency can help your child be more comfortable. *Very specific* means that you do and say the same things every time you drop her off and pick her up. For example, park in the same area, enter through the same door, approach the cubby, hang up the coat, check the job chart and comment on the day's assignment, give two hugs and two kisses, and say, "See ya later, alligator!"

- **Let your child know when you will return each day.** It's comforting for a child to know that you will be there at a certain time. Tie in your arrival with a specific activity, such as after snack time, and let your child know when to expect you.
- **Schedule an adjustment period.** When you drop off your child and again when you pick her up, allow a five-minute adjustment period. (The time is worth it, as you'll save at least fifteen minutes of fussing!) When you arrive at the day-care center, allow your child to play or show you something for five minutes. When it's time to leave, use a fun indicator, such as a tickle on the neck. Or, hold up your key ring and have it tell your child (in a funny voice) that the car is waiting and ready to go.
- **Have a fun routine for the drive home.** Leave a snack bag on your child's seat with different contents every day, such as graham crackers, dry cereal, pretzels, or fruit. Play a certain game in the parking lot as you walk to the car, such as counting all the red cars you see or counting your steps. Mention something that your child can look forward to at home, such as reading the new library books or Grandpa coming for dinner.

What Not to Do

- **Don't cater to the complaints.** If you try too hard to convince her that everything is okay, you may just make her nervous. Instead, stay lighthearted and have confidence that everything will be fine. Most children stop crying within five minutes of a parent's departure. Ask your day-care provider if this is true for your child. If you like, call the center when you get to work or arrive at home so they can reassure you that your child has finished crying and is playing happily.
- **Don't get mad.** Your anger will just make your child fuss and cry even more, and it won't solve a thing. Moreover, it's also a very unpleasant way to start the day (for both of you).

Doesn't Come When Called

See also: Dawdling

> Even if I call my child four or five times, he still won't respond to me. It's like he's wearing earplugs! If I want him to come at all I usually have to go get him.

Think About It

Your child has learned exactly what you've taught him—that he doesn't have to heed your calls. He knows that if you really do want him—you'll come and get him.

What to Do

• **Call. Wait. Act.** Follow this procedure: Visually locate your child. Call once. Wait three minutes. Go to your child, take him by the hand, and say, "When I call, I would like you to come." Then lead him to the desired location. If you do this consistently, he will know that you really do expect him to come when called.

• **Watch how the adults in your family act.** Does the caller yell from two rooms away? Does the callee mumble, "In a minute," and then have to be reminded several times before responding? These are the models for your child's behavior. Change the ways you respond to each other, and model the behavior that you want of your child.

• **Give a warning.** Making a transition from one activity to another can be difficult for children. Instead of calling, "Come now!" try giving two warnings first. "You'll need to come in five minutes." A few minutes later, say, "Two minutes." Then, "Please come in now." At this point, wait a minute. If he doesn't respond, go to him and take him by the hand saying, "When I call I would like you to come."

- **Acknowledge your child's desires.** Let him know that you understand he wants to continue playing, and then follow with a statement and an action that promotes compliance, such as "I bet you wish you could stay in the pool forever, but it's time to go now. Here's your towel."

- **Use a dinner bell or timer to call your child.** Tell him that when he hears the bell, he needs to come before you count to fifty. This is a fun and specific indicator. If you have more than one child, you can let the first one to respond to your call ring the bell a second time.

- **Check his hearing.** Make sure that your child has had a hearing test and that his failure to respond isn't because of a hearing problem.

What Not to Do

- **Don't call to your child from more than twenty feet away.** The farther you are from your child, the more likely he'll ignore your calls.

- **Don't call your child until you're *really* ready for him to come.** If you summon your child but then get involved in something else, you are reinforcing that your call is only a warning that you'll need him sometime soon.

Hitting a Parent

See also: Biting, Child to Adult

> When my child is angry, he sometimes shoves or hits me. I've tried to explain to him that he shouldn't, but he keeps doing it.

Think About It

Children typically hit because they are frustrated, don't get their way, and can't get their point across. However, hitting an adult is a serious offense and should be treated as such. It must be nipped in the bud. This is as much about establishing control in the relationship as it is about teaching how to handle emotions and how to show respect for other human beings.

What to Do

- **Respond naturally.** Many children are unaware of how other people feel or how their actions affect others. It is through experience that they learn best. If your child hits you, respond with an "Ouch! That hurts!" Then explain that it isn't the way to get your attention, saying, "Use your words to tell me what you want."
- **Respond instantly.** Every time your child hits you, immediately take him gently by the hands, look him in the eye, and say in a firm, no-nonsense voice, "No hitting! Time-out." Guide the child to a chair or other time-out place and announce, "Stay here."

Madeline, age 6, and Isabella, age 3

After a few minutes, when both you and your child have calmed down, you can give your child permission to get up. At that point, briefly remind your child of what happened and ask for an apology. Avoid a long follow-up lecture. It's more important to respond quickly and appropriately each time your child hits.

• **Stop playtime slaps.** Children will do as they see done, even though they may do it at inappropriate times. If you are in the habit of playfully roughhousing with your child and allowing him to hit you in fun, he may find it difficult to draw the line between the play behavior and the angry behavior.

• **Talk to a professional if you need help.** If your child continues to hit you after you've taken measures to stop the behavior, it may be time to talk to a family counselor or therapist. A trained professional can determine the reasons your child is hitting and help your family work out a plan to stop the behavior.

What Not to Do

- **Don't respond in a timid voice or with a lengthy lecture.** Neither accurately communicates the severity of the misbehavior, nor does either teach your child how to handle his anger appropriately.
- **Don't hit back.** This can be an almost subconscious response, but it obviously doesn't teach the intended lesson. How can you teach him not to hit people when you are hitting people?

Hitting, Kicking, and Hair Pulling

....

See also: Biting Other Children; Sibling Fights

> When my daughter gets angry at a friend, she hits or grabs a fistful of hair and yanks. I've lectured her and yelled at her, but it doesn't seem to help.

Think About It

Hair pulling, kicking, biting, and hitting are all typical emotional behaviors of young children. They may act this way because of a lack of knowledge and self-control. It is not a sign that your child is hateful or mean. Children are human beings, and human beings *will* get angry, we can't prevent that. It's up to us to teach our children how to handle their frustration and anger in socially appropriate ways.

What to Do

- **Intercede before it happens.** Watch your child closely during playtime. When you see her becoming frustrated or angry, take the time to intervene. Coach her through the issue by teaching her how to handle her frustrations. Teach her what to do, or model what to say to her friend. Or if she seems too upset to learn at that moment, redirect her attention to another activity until her emotions level out.

Mother-Speak

"My daughter, Gracie, would sometimes hit her little friend when they were playing together. Of course Gracie never intended to hit her, but when she got overly excited or wanted a toy, she would hit. Recently I've tried 'talking it up' before the play date starts. 'Gracie, in a few minutes, Caitlyn is coming over to play. Remember that you need to be very gentle with Caitlyn. You give her hugs. You share your toys with her. Be nice to Caitlyn, and no hitting. Hitting hurts. Hitting makes Caitlyn cry. You need to be gentle, okay?' I just keep repeating myself over and over again, and she will repeat back a few of my sentences as if reciting a mantra of some sort! And lo and behold—the times I've done this, there's been no hitting."

—Sarah, mother to Gracie, age 2, and Sam, age 9 months

• **Teach your child how to express anger or frustration respectfully.** It's one thing to tell a child what not to do or to step into an argument. It's another thing entirely to teach her what to do in advance of the next problem. This can be done through role-play, discussion, and reading children's books about angry emotions together.

• **Examine any hidden causes.** Is your child hungry, tired, sick, jealous, frustrated, or scared? If you can identify any feelings driving your child's actions, you can address those along with the aggressive behavior.

• **Give more attention to the injured party.** Often the child who hits or kicks gets so much attention that the action becomes a way of gaining the spotlight. Instead, give more attention to the child who was hurt. Make only a brief statement, like "No hair pulling!" Then turn and give your attention to the child whose hair was pulled. "Come here, honey. Mommy will give you a hug and read you a book."

- **Show how to use positive physical touches.** Show your child how to hold hands during a walk or how to give a backrub or foot massage. Teach a few physical games, such as tag or leap frog. Under direct supervision, children who are more physical can gain a positive outlet for their physical energy.

- **Teach your child to clap her hands together whenever she feels an urge to hit.** This gives her an immediate physical outlet for her angry emotions and helps her learn to keep her hands to herself. An alternate is to teach her to put her hands in her pockets whenever she feels like hitting. Reward with praise anytime you see her doing this successfully.

- **Give your child a time-out when needed.** Every time your child acts out aggressively, immediately and gently take the child by the shoulders, look her in the eye, and say in a firm voice, "No hurting others, time out." Guide the child to a chair or other time-out place and tell her, "You may get up when you can play without hitting." By telling her that she can get up when *she's* ready, you let her know that *she* is responsible for controlling her behavior. If your child gets up and hits again, say, "You are not ready to get up yet," and direct her back to a time-out.

- **Avoid play hitting and wrestling.** Young children who hit, wrestle, or roughhouse with a parent or sibling during playtime might use these same actions during nonwrestling times. It can be hard for them to draw the line between the two. If you have a child who has trouble controlling her physical acts, then avoid this kind of play.

What Not to Do

- **Don't lose control and yell, hit, or grab your child roughly.** When you see your child hurting another person it's easy to fly off the handle. Getting angry, though, won't teach your child what she needs to learn: how to control her emotions when others are making her mad. You are mad at her, so she'll be watching how you handle your anger.

- **Don't focus on punishment.** More than anything your child needs instructions on how to treat other human beings, particularly during moments of anger or frustration.

- **Don't let your child watch TV shows or movies that involve hitting or other violence.** Children can become immune to the impact of the violence. Studies tell us that children copy what they see on TV, which often portrays aggression as an appropriate way of handling anger.

- **Don't assume your child can figure it out.** If your child comes to you asking for help in dealing with a difficult situation, don't send her away for tattling. She may then return to the situation angry and express her emotions inappropriately. View her call for help as an invitation to teach her important social skills.

Interrupting

See also: Manners; Mealtime Behavior

> My husband and I haven't had an uninterrupted
> conversation since our twins started talking! The boys
> interrupt us constantly.

Think About It

Your children interrupt you because they get a response from you when they do. They've learned that you are always willing to stop what you're doing to answer them. Children often are so focused on their own needs that they don't realize you also have needs at that moment. They need to learn how to pay attention to other people's needs as well as their own.

What to Do

• **Give lessons and examples.** Since they may have a hard time deciphering when interruptions are justified, teach your children how to determine if something warrants an interruption. Discuss examples of times when it's okay to interrupt—for example, when someone is at the door or on the phone or if a sibling is hurt.

• **Coach the proper manners.** Teach your child how to wait for a pause in the conversation and to say, "Excuse me." When he remembers to do this, respond positively to him. If the interruption is of a nature that it can and should wait, politely inform your child of this.

• **Teach "the squeeze."** Tell your child that if he wants something when you are talking to another adult, he should walk up to you and gently squeeze your arm. You will then squeeze his hand to indicate that you know he is there and will be with him in a minute. At first, respond rather quickly so your child can see the success of this method. Over time you can wait longer; just give a gentle squeeze every few minutes to remind your child that you remember the request.

• **Create a busy box.** Put together a box of activities or games that can only be used when you are on the telephone, working at your desk, or talking with an adult. Occasionally refill it with new things or rotate the contents. Be firm about putting the box and

Sage, 10 months; Ethan, age 7; and Devan, age 2½

its contents away when you are done. Your child will look forward to your next conversation, which will be interruption free!

- **Plan ahead.** Before you make a phone call or have a visitor, let your child know what to expect. "I'm going to make a phone call. I'll be a while, so let's get your busy box ready to use while I'm on the phone."
- **Commend your child when it is deserved.** Praise your child for using good manners, for remembering to say, "Excuse me," and for interrupting only for a valid reason.

What Not to Do

- **Don't answer the interruption.** Many parents admonish their children for interrupting but in the same breath respond to the child's interrupted request, which just reinforces the habit.
- **Don't be rude.** Parents sometimes jump in so quickly to correct their child's bad manners that they don't realize that the way in which their correction is delivered is itself rude. ("What is the matter with you? Stop interrupting us!") Use your own good manners to model appropriate communication skills. Pause, look at your child, and say, "I'll be with you in a minute."

Lying

Lately I've been catching my son in small lies, such as "I didn't do it." I know that he did, but I'm reluctant to call him a liar.

Think About It

It is a good idea to avoid tagging a child with any unpleasant label. Children form opinions of who they are, and we don't want them to view themselves in such a negative way. We do, however, want to deal with this behavior whenever it happens, teach our children about honesty, and prevent lying from becoming a habit. Children don't tell the truth for a number of different reasons. They lie so they won't get in trouble, they lie to cover embarrassment, or they lie because they don't make the distinction between fact and fiction. Mainly, they lie because they don't understand the importance of always telling the truth. Teaching your child the value of telling the truth takes time, teaching, consistency, and patience.

What to Do

- **Make telling the truth a recognized family value.** Children learn what traits are important to you by your words and actions. Choose those values that are most important to you, such as being truthful, and discuss them with your child from time to time. You can point out the subject when it comes up in books, in movies, or in life experiences.

- **Focus on finding a solution instead of laying blame.** When your child makes a mistake and comes forward with the truth, resist the urge to yell or punish. Instead, involve him in finding solutions. "Regardless of how it happened, the lamp is broken. What are we going to do about it?"
- **Set reasonable expectations.** Children sometimes lie because they feel they're not meeting your expectations, and they think it's easier to lie than disappoint you. Take a look at how you respond to your child's mistakes or inadequacies, and make sure you leave room for imperfections.
- **Teach your child to take responsibility for his mistakes.** If you witness him doing something wrong, coach your child to say, "I was wrong. I'm sorry." This is something many adults still have trouble doing—so start him young. People who are comfortable admitting their mistakes are less likely to lie to cover them up.
- **Model truthfulness.** When your child hears you telling "little white lies," you are teaching your child something important about lies and honesty. Model what you hope to see from your child.

What Not to Do

- **Don't ask questions that set your child up to lie.** When your child has chocolate on his face and the candy wrapper is on the table, don't ask, "Did you eat the candy that was on the counter?" Instead make a statement of fact: "It appears that you ate the candy without asking."
- **Don't assume something is a lie if you are not sure.** If you suspect your child isn't telling the truth but you're not 100 percent

sure, don't accuse him of lying. *But* do express your concern: "That doesn't sound like the truth to me."

• **Don't assume your child is lying to be naughty.** Your child may be afraid to confess what he's done for fear of punishment or of disappointing you. That's different from purposely lying to deceive you.

Manners

See also: Bossiness; Interrupting; Mealtime Behavior;
Restaurant Behavior

> My son has bad manners—he doesn't even remember
> the basics, to say "please" and "thank you."

Think About It

Your child doesn't run into the freeway or play with steak knives
because you've made it clear that these behaviors won't be toler-
ated. You must decide that using good manners is just as important
for him to learn. Children aren't born with proper manners. They
must be taught about manners and then consistently reminded.

What to Do

- **Tell him exactly what you'd like to hear.** Rephrase what
your child has said in the way you find acceptable. "What I'd like
to hear you say is, 'May I please have more pancakes?' "
- **Teach instead of chastise.** Instead of saying, "That's horrible!" respond in a positive, teaching way. "It's impolite to belch
at the table, and if you do, it's proper to say, 'Excuse me.' " If your
child didn't know what the proper behavior was, you're teaching a
valuable lesson. If he did, you're displaying *your* good manners as
you correct him.

- **Model the behavior you'd like to see.** It's easy for a parent to forget to use "please," "thank you," and "excuse me" when dealing with young children. Remember your manners. It's easy teaching, and it makes life more pleasant. So, replace "Stop making that noise" with "Please play quietly."
- **Praise your child.** Show your appreciation when your child uses good manners.

What Not to Do

- **Don't respond to bad manners.** Look your child in the eye and say, "I know that you have nice manners. When you can ask me using your good manners, I'll be happy to answer you."

Mother-Speak

"I've discovered that simple modeling often brings about the behavior I'm hoping for. I have always said 'thank you' when my daughter handed me something. She started saying it, and now she almost always says 'thank you' when something is given to her. When I wanted her to start saying 'please,' I tried the 'Say please for Mommy' and 'Where are your manners?' route and got nowhere. Then I gave up and just started making sure I said 'please' to her all the time, and it worked! She now says 'please' consistently. Now I've incorporated this form of teaching into everything else. It's not instant and not perfect, but it works. Plus, I have a cheerful, confident, happy little girl I get to enjoy because I'm not constantly frustrated in a mommy-child tug of power."

—Sheri, mother to Faith, age 2

- **Don't laugh at bad manners.** Laughing encourages children to see dreadful manners as a source of humor.
- **Don't use those old-school responses.** "Waad-do-ya-say?" or "Where are your manners?" aren't very polite ways to remind your child to use his manners.

Mealtime Behavior

See also: Interrupting; Manners

My son won't sit still for a meal. He's up and down,
picks food off his plate, and doesn't use good
table manners.

Think About It

Children have an abundance of energy, so sitting still for any
length of time such as at a meal is a challenge. Moreover, children
don't find social pleasure in sharing a meal (they'd rather play), and
food itself is not a priority for them (unless it's ice cream).

What to Do

• **Be patient and teach.** Tell your child what you want, rather
than what you don't want. Avoid saying, "Don't eat with your
hands!" Instead, tell him what you do want: "Please use your
fork."

• **Keep a happy mood at the table.** Focus on pleasant conversation; don't use the time to reprimand. Don't let adults dominate
the dinner conversation and continually shush the children. Allow
children to take part in the conversation, too. Make mealtime a
joyful family time with everyone sharing.

• **Accept age-appropriate behavior.** All children spill their
milk, splatter their ketchup, and leave an array of crumbs around

their chairs. It takes time to acquire the motor skills required to be tidy and clean.

- **Be consistent.** Require children to use the good manners that you've taught them. Children who routinely practice using good manners will adopt those manners as good habits.
- **Practice formal manners.** Every once in a while, have a formal meal. Use a tablecloth (an old one!) and a full selection of silverware and napkins. Pretend you're at a fancy restaurant, and allow everyone to exaggerate his or her best manners. You may even choose to dress up and use candles. In addition to teaching good manners, it's a beautiful family ritual and will create wonderful memories.

What Not to Do

- **Don't have unrealistic expectations.** If you expect your young child to sit quietly at the table for a long meal and use impeccable manners, you are setting yourself up for disappointment. Children aren't little adults.
- **Don't force your child to eat when he's not hungry.** Children have natural appetite control. They should be allowed to eat when they are hungry and stop when they are full. Allow your child to continue to listen to his body. If you require your child to clean his plate, use a smaller plate and child-sized servings. One caveat here: your child might not differentiate between cookies and broccoli, so you need to provide healthy choices.

Messiness

My child leaves toys, socks, tissues, and dishes lying around the house and expects me to clean up after him.

Think About It

As parents, we set ourselves up for this one, I'm afraid. One day we have a baby who requires our total care, and the next thing we know we are still providing the same level of care to a six-year-old who's never had a compelling reason to want life any other way. If you had a live-in maid who followed you around and tidied up all your messes, I bet you'd be pleased to let her continue to do it, too!

What to Do

- **Be consistent.** If some days you encourage your child to clean up but other days you ignore the mess, your child won't have a clear expectation of what you want him to do. Set a plan and stick to it.

- **Create a daily routine for cleaning up.** One day's mess is usually manageable, but a mess that adds up day after day becomes insurmountable. Pick a scheduled time that you can adhere to every day, such as after dinner or before putting on pajamas, for a daily cleanup.

- **Join in during the cleanup time.** Cleaning up together makes it more pleasant. Over time this cleanup routine will become habit and your child will cooperate with little fuss.
- **Get more organized.** Make sure there is a place for everything, and teach your child to keep everything in its rightful place. Use plastic bins, boxes, and shelves to stay organized.

What Not to Do

- **Don't constantly clean up after your child.** If your child never participates in cleaning up, he won't learn how to do it.
- **Don't complain about it.** If your child doesn't have a cleanup routine and you don't have clear expectations, then it's not his fault that you're unhappy. Instead of complaining, use your energy to teach good habits.

Other People's Undisciplined Children

See also: Biting Other Children; Bossiness;
Playtime Behavior

I have a close friend I've always enjoyed spending
time with. The problem is that her children are
boisterous and disobedient, and she does nothing to
correct them.

Think About It

When you love your friend and she loves her children but your parenting styles are very different, it becomes a very sensitive issue. Chances are she doesn't see her children the same way you do. Tread lightly when you approach issues about other people's children because lifelong friendships can be broken over contrasting parenting approaches.

What to Do

• **Use distraction and redirection.** If you see a problem brewing, step in and invite the children to get involved in an activity. Keeping them busy may help avoid confrontation or problems.

• **Focus only on the issue at hand.** Find a solution to the current problem only, don't address personality or lifestyle. Do what's necessary to get through the visit. Make your comments about the action or the group, not the individual child.

• **Share parenting knowledge in a nonthreatening way.** Invite your friend to accompany you to a parenting class or to attend a lecture. Share a copy of your favorite parenting book—tell her that you love it and you're sure she will, too.

• **Pick your battles.** Try to take pleasure in your visits and overlook the petty issues. Focus on the things you enjoy about your friend, and open your heart to finding some things to enjoy in her children, as well.

• **Have childfree visits.** If her children's behavior affects your own children or causes too much stress for you, then schedule mainly adults-only social events.

What Not to Do

• **Don't parent other people's children.** Allow your friend to deal with her children's behavior (or not deal with it, as the case may be). Get involved only when something involves your children or your property.

• **Don't think you can change other people.** Don't expend energy thinking you can change your friend's family life with a few well-placed comments. Forcing change on others can make them hurt, angry, or defensive. Furthermore, unless she asks for help she may be content with things as they are.

• **Don't stop seeing your friend.** Friendships are precious and important to your health and happiness. Children eventually mature and grow up, and you won't be around her children as much as they get older. Find ways to make this situation work for you.

Playtime Behavior

....

See also: Biting Other Children;
Hitting, Kicking, and Hair Pulling; Other People's
Undisciplined Children

> I joined a play group with the idea that my
> preschooler would have fun playing with other
> children. But it's usually not fun because they don't
> share, they bicker, and they all have crying spells—
> my son included.

Think About It

Developing friendship skills takes time and experience. The only way children learn social skills is by practice, so even though there are plenty of bumps along the way it's worth scheduling playtime with other children.

What to Do

- **Have realistic expectations.** Young and inexperienced children will need guidance during playtime. Even with supervision, children will get into tussles with each other—and if they didn't they'd never learn how to handle the disagreements that are a part of life. Look at these moments as golden teaching opportunities.
- **Watch for signs of hunger or tiredness.** Children lose patience and good humor when they are tired or hungry. If hunger is the issue, supply a wholesome snack to the group. If tiredness

Treston, age 2

hits, either leave for home or pull out a quiet game or a favorite movie for the children to watch together.

- **Choose the right activities.** Sharing toys can be a challenge, so avoid having just a few special toys to pass among the group. Good choices for group play are things like building blocks, art projects, and imaginative play supplies such as dress-up clothes and toy kitchen supplies. Having several different activities to choose from can help, also.

- **Coach them through problems.** Children can get frustrated or angry with a friend, but they don't have the self-control or wisdom to handle their frustrations in the proper way. You'll need to teach the kids how to negotiate and compromise when they have a problem. Ask each one in turn to explain what happened. Then guide them through solving the problem.

- **Listen and watch.** You don't have to mediate every argument. Often children will work through a disagreement on their own. Step in only if the argument continues with no sense of resolution in sight, or if they begin to push or hit each other.
- **Praise and encourage.** When your child has had a good play session, don't be shy about giving out compliments. Let your child know that you're proud of him or her.

What Not to Do

- **Don't make play dates too long.** Children's social skills tend to deteriorate over time. Watch your child for signs that it's time to end the event. One to three hours is usually plenty for young children. As they get more familiar and comfortable in the friendship, you can experiment with longer playtimes.
- **Don't force friendships on children who don't mesh.** Just like adults, some children click and play well together. Others seem to clash whenever they are together. Try to choose playmates that bring out the best in your child.
- **Don't leave the children alone while the adults socialize.** When children are older you'll be able to leave them alone to play. Younger children, though, require more monitoring and supervision to keep things running smoothly.
- **Don't have too large a group.** If you are having behavior problems, see what happens if you pare down to only two or three children at a time. The more little personalities in the room, the more likely problems will arise. Once you notice that things are consistently going well in the small group, then you can move on to a bigger play group.

Restaurant Behavior

See also: Interrupting; Manners; Mealtime Behavior

We like to go out to eat with our children, but even a meal at a fast-food restaurant is exhausting. Every time we go out, we end up wishing we'd stayed home and ordered pizza.

Think About It

Children can be both excited and bored at a restaurant. Also, they can find it difficult to sit in one place for the length of time necessary to order, wait, eat, and pay for the meal. This problem is one that improves with age, development, and practice. With a good game plan, you can help your children learn how to behave appropriately in a restaurant so that you can all enjoy the experience.

What to Do

- **Pick the right restaurant.** Choose a restaurant based on its level of child-friendliness. Consider the availability of a children's menu that includes food your children will actually eat, the absence of a long wait for a table, and booster seats or high chairs. Private booths or eating nooks as opposed to one large open room can make dining out more fun. And a noisier, family-friendly atmosphere can help.

- **Teach restaurant manners at home.** If you are casual about mealtime manners at home, don't expect your children to miraculously develop table manners because you happen to be sitting in a restaurant. Practice good manners at home for every meal, and your children will be prepared when you eat out.

- **Have longer sit-down meals at home.** Typically, at home we call our children to the table when the food is ready and then excuse them as soon as they are finished eating. If you want to practice for restaurant visits, it's a good idea to have them come to the table a few minutes earlier. Then sit and chat for a bit after you are finished with the meal. Make it fun by telling stories or jokes or talking about upcoming plans. Not only will this be great practice for eating out, it's a wonderful ritual to introduce into your home.

- **Dine out at your regular mealtime.** When possible, stick close to your routine. Plan to dine at a reasonable time, before your children become famished and tired. If you must go out later than your usual time, provide your children with a snack at the normal time and allow them to have a smaller meal at the restaurant, or to eat half the restaurant meal and bring the rest home.

- **Review your restaurant rules before you go.** Be very specific, and leave no stone unturned. A sample list of "restaurant rules" might be: Sit in your seat. Use a quiet inside voice. Use your silverware, not your fingers. Have nice conversation; no bickering. If you don't like something, keep your comments to yourself and fill up on something else. If you have to use the restroom, ask me privately and I'll take you.

- **Ask for an immediate appetizer.** Many restaurants automatically bring bread or chips to the table as soon as you are seated. If this isn't the case, ask for something to be brought out for the children to nibble on.

- **Prevent boredom.** Bring along a few simple toys such as a deck of cards, plastic animals, or small quiet toys that can keep children occupied while they wait.

> **Mother-Speak**
>
> "We ask for to-go boxes and the check at the same time we order our food. This way, if we have to leave because of a tired or whiny child, we can make a fast getaway."
>
> **—Reagan, mother to Hailey, age 2**

What Not to Do

- **Don't imagine that eating out *with* children is the same as dining *without* them.** When you take children to a restaurant, the focus is not the cuisine or the atmosphere. It's all about controlling the excitement and boredom, teaching your children formal manners, and having quality family time.

- **Don't stay too long after eating.** Keep your post-meal conversation short. The longer you stay, the more likely your children will run out of patience and act up.

- **Don't make them eat what they don't like.** Stick with familiar foods when possible. If the grilled cheese sandwich your child ordered turns out to be Swiss cheese on sourdough, allow your child to eat the French fries and pack up the sandwich. A restaurant is not the place to battle over new and unfamiliar foods.

- **Don't stay if you're not having fun.** If a child's behavior gets out of hand, take her to the restroom or out to the car for a time-out. If she continues to misbehave, don't be afraid to ask for doggie bags and leave the restaurant. But don't give up. Review your expectations and try again.

Roughhousing or Wild Play

See also: Sibling Fights; Yelling, Screaming, and Shouting

When my children play they like to wrestle, chase, and shout. They're noisy and rambunctious. I don't have a lot of patience for this, so I usually end up yelling at them to stop.

Think About It

Children have an abundance of energy—and it's a good thing. We just need to help them find the right outlets for that energy.

What to Do

• **Move them to another place.** If the problem is the *location* of the play more than the play itself, just shift the setting. When you see the children begin to get physically active, move them outside or to a room that is safe for rough-and-tumble activity.

• **Stop the play before it gets out of hand.** Perhaps you repeatedly admonish your children to "be careful" or "settle down" but let things progress until something is broken or someone is hurt. Only then do you actually put a stop to the action. Instead, step in when you sense that things are headed in the wrong direction and divert their attention to a different activity.

- **Provide optional entertainment.** Sometimes children start roughhousing if they are bored and not being creative about finding something to do. Put together an easily accessible "activity closet" with games, crafts, puzzles, art supplies, and other activities that can help to absorb their energies.

What Not to Do

- **Don't yell.** Adding your loud voice to an already intense situation won't help your children calm down or find something productive to do.
- **Don't threaten.** Don't make empty threats like "If you don't stop right now, then I'll. . . ." These statements undermine your authority and assume disobedience. Moreover, these threats usually aren't carried out and your children know that, so they don't encourage the cooperation you're hoping for. The only thing threats tend to do is create negative energy. Try to stick to instructions that tell your children what you *do* want them to do.

Sharing

See also: Biting Other Children; Hitting, Kicking, and Hair Pulling; Sibling Fights

> My child has a hard time sharing her toys
> with others.

Think About It

Sharing is a complicated social skill that takes guidance and practice to develop. Young children get very attached to their possessions, and they don't understand how sharing will affect them or their toy. In order to get a better understanding of these feelings, think for a minute about one of your most prized or important possessions—perhaps your computer, camera, car, or boat. Now think of having a friend take it away to use for a day. That feeling of apprehension and uncertainty, plus inexperience, may be at the root of your child's reluctance to share.

What to Do

- **Demonstrate how to share.** Share things with your child and point out that you are sharing. For example, "Would you like a turn on my calculator? I'd be happy to share it with you."
- **Encourage your child to share toys with you.** It's often easier for a child to share with a parent, since the child knows you'll be careful and that you'll give the toy back when you're done.

It makes for good sharing practice. When you hand her toy back, explain what she just did. "You shared so nicely, thank you." That way she has a good feeling about what it means to share, since her young friends probably won't treat it the same way.

- **Give your child choices.** Instead of demanding that your child share a specific toy, give her some options. "Sarah would like to play with a stuffed animal. Which one would you like to let her play with?"
- **Create situations that require sharing.** Your child can get good practice with sharing when given toys or games that require two or more people to play, such as board games or yard games (such as badminton). Also look for activities that have plenty of opportunities for everyone to participate, such as modeling clay, coloring or art projects, or building blocks.

Arianna, age 2, and Mommy

Mother-Speak

"My children were constantly fighting over toys, even if there were two identical ones. My husband bought one of those label-making machines, and now if one of the children has a special toy, we label it. My son, Daniel, is into spelling things right now, so he types his name into the label maker, prints it out, and sticks the label on his toy. We help my daughter label her toys, too. They both beam at seeing their names on their special things, and they respect each other's toys as well."

—Ezia, mother to Daniel, age 4, and Sedona, age 2

- **Let your child know what to expect prior to a sharing situation.** Before a friend's visit, let her know how long the friend will be there and reassure her that all her things will still be hers after the friend leaves. Allow your child to put away a few favorite things that do not have to be shared. Never require a child to share a special toy that is a frequent plaything or bedtime companion.
- **Praise good sharing moments.** Watch for good things that happen—no matter how briefly—and praise your child for sharing nicely.

What Not to Do

- **Don't shame your child for not sharing.** If your child isn't willing to share, she needs to learn more about the process. Teach, rather than punish.
- **Don't embarrass your child with a public reprimand.** Even if you've given lessons, prepared your child, and set up a good situ-

ation for sharing, your child might still refuse to share. When this happens, take her to another room, discuss the issue privately, and set a plan for how the rest of her playtime should progress.

• **Don't force your child to share special toys, gifts, or "lovies."** Some things should be exempt from sharing rules, such as a favorite doll, a stuffed animal she sleeps with, a fragile toy, or a gift recently given to her.

Shopping Misbehavior

See also: Backtalk; Car Problems; Dawdling; Doesn't Come When Called

> I have to go shopping once or twice a week, and I have to take my child with me. He hates to go, and so he usually ends up begging for candy and then fussing, crying, or having a tantrum in the store.

Think About It

Often it's not shopping that young children object to, but the stressful, businesslike approach parents adopt when running errands. In addition, many adult events are uninteresting to children and the length of most shopping excursions tends to exceed a child's limited amount of patience.

What to Do

- **View shopping trips as events rather than errands.** This is a great time to achieve two things at once: get your shopping done and have some quality time with your child. If you are a busy, multitasking parent, you'll find this mind-set helps you have a more patient, pleasant attitude, which will easily rub off on your child.
- **Plan more time to shop.** When you are not in a rush, you and your child will be more relaxed and have a more pleasant time. If you must hurry, make a list in advance and stick to it.

Roaming the store for random purchases makes it a much longer trip.

- **Engage your child.** Most children love to be helpers at the store. They can carry things to the cart, choose produce, and find items on the shelves. Children who can read might enjoy having their own short list of items to find.
- **Ask your child for input.** When you can, pick two similar items and ask your child which one you should buy. Having a say in what you put into the cart is very exciting and empowering for children.
- **Acknowledge your child's desires.** "Yummy. Those cookies do look good." Follow this with a statement of why you'll not be buying it, without sounding reproving—for example, "But we're not buying any cookies today."

Mother-Speak

"I did an experiment with my son one day. I decided (without telling him) to let him lead us through our shopping experience. I had no schedule for the day, and we were just out for fun. He walked and I followed. He found all kinds of things that were interesting to him, and I found lots I wanted to see, too. Unfortunately, he 'made me keep moving' to get where he wanted to go. I found myself wanting to wander off or go home, but we stayed until he wanted to leave. It was an excruciatingly painful experience and a test of my patience, but it made me realize what children go through as they are dragged along on countless uninteresting errands with busy adults."

—Janell, mother to Allen, age 4, and Megan, age 2

Mother-Speak

"When we're shopping I let my boys choose one treat, but they often ask for more after that. I very nicely say, 'Sure, you can have fruit roll-ups instead of the cookies you chose earlier—let's go put the cookies back.' Suddenly, there's no more clamoring for the fruit roll-ups."

—Judith, mother to Robbie, age 11; Harry, age 6; and Elizabeth, age 9 months

- **Create a written or an imaginary wish list.** Whenever your child says, "I want this," tell him that you will remember that he likes it. You can even jot it down on paper and call it his wish list.

- **Prevent the constant gimmees.** Let your child know in advance what you will or will not be buying that day before you enter the store. If you can allow him to choose one treat to put in the basket each time you shop, he will know not to ask for an endless list of things. Having to decide on his one thing also gives him a purpose for the trip.

- **Have consistent rules.** If you shop frequently, it will help to write on a note card the top five or six shopping rules and put the note card in the car. Each time before you shop, review the rules with your children.

What Not to Do

- **Don't take a hungry child grocery shopping.** You might not intentionally plan this, but it happens. If it has been an hour or two since your child last ate, the first item on your list should be a snack your child can eat as you shop. A box of crackers, a bag of pretzels, or a corn dog can work wonders to take the edge off. (Just remember to pay for it when checking out.)

• **Don't take a tired child shopping.** Avoid scheduling shopping trips too close to nap time. Tired children are absolutely more fussy and impatient.

• **Don't shop at the store's busiest hours.** When possible schedule your shopping times to avoid the largest crowds. More people in the store mean longer lines and more complications. A quiet, less-populated store will also help you feel less stressed. A cashier or manager can recommend good shopping times.

Sibling Fights

See also: Biting Other Children; Bossiness; Hitting, Kicking, and Hair Pulling; Playtime Behavior

It really bothers me when my children fight with each other. I want them to be friends!

Think About It

When our children fight, it not only grates on our nerves, it tugs on our hearts. We want them to love each other, and we want them to build lifelong friendships. When they quarrel it seems this will never happen. In reality, all siblings fight with each other and it is not a measure of their love or their friendship—it's the normal development of social and relationship skills. The vast majority of sibling battles are not destructive to the relationship between the children. All this considered, there *are* ways to reduce the number of fights and the severity of them, as well.

What to Do

- **Identify and solve the problems.** Try to determine if there is a pattern to your children's fights. *Do they typically fight over one thing, such as sharing toys?* If so, make rules about sharing. *Do they always fight while you're making dinner?* You could enlist their help in preparing the meal, feed them a healthy snack, or have an activity planned during that time, such as coloring or playing with clay. *Do they fight while they are getting ready for bed in the evening?* Create and follow a peaceful bedtime routine that occurs earlier in the evening before the nighttime meltdown occurs. The idea here is to identify the "hot spots" between your children and create a plan to prevent the problem from continually causing arguments.

• **Teach.** Teach your children how to talk, negotiate, and compromise with each other. They are likely to be blinded by their own side of the story and need help to see each other's point of view. You can even have your children sit on a sofa together, or on adjacent chairs, to talk. Rather than dictating a resolution, help them discuss the problem and come to the best conclusion. Over time, and with practice, they will learn how to settle arguments on their own.

• **Distract.** If the argument is over a trivial issue, you can often defuse the tension with humor or distract the children with another activity.

• **Praise good behavior.** It frequently happens that when children are playing together nicely the parent takes advantage of the peace to catch up on some work. Then, when a fight breaks out, the parent shows up to solve the problem. So, don't disregard your children when they are getting along well! Reward them for getting

Mother-Speak

"Recently I've been dealing with Kekoa being less than nice to his little brother. It's really frustrating because the mama bear comes out in me each time he knocks Kalani down or takes a toy away from him. I've been telling myself I need to be calmer and nicer about how I handle those situations, and to be patient and teach. Kindness begets kindness, I think."

—**Michel, mother to Kekoa, age 3, and Kalani, age 1**

along with some positive attention. Make a comment of appreciation, such as, "I'm happy that you enjoy playing together." Giving attention when things are going well will confirm your expectations and encourage them to continue the positive behavior.

What Not to Do

- **Don't assume that only one child is at fault.** Don't assume that your older child controls the relationship. Don't assume that a more aggressive child is always at fault. Sometimes one child has taunted or teased the sibling to the point of frustration. It's important to be aware of any behind-the-scenes ordeals that may be testing one child's patience to its limit.
- **Don't assume there's nothing you can do.** Yes, siblings fight. But they can learn from you how to handle their disagreements in a respectful way.

Sleep Issues—Bedtime

See also: Sleep Issues—Naps

> Our daughter hates bedtime. It's a battle every night to get her into bed, and then she's up several times during the night.

Think About It

Up to 70 percent of children under age six have sleep problems. Sleep issues are complicated and have many different causes. They're hard to deal with because when children aren't sleeping, parents aren't sleeping, either. Lack of sleep affects *every minute* of *every day* because lack of sleep isn't just about being tired. Sleep has a role in everything—dawdling, temper tantrums, hyperactivity, growth, health, and even learning. Improving your child's sleep patterns can bring more peace to your home.

What to Do

- **Maintain a consistent time for going to bed and waking up.** Your child's biological clock has an influence on her wakefulness and sleepiness. When you establish a set time for bedtime and wake-up time, you "set" your child's clock so that it functions smoothly.
- **Aim for an early bedtime.** Most children will sleep *better* and *longer* when they go to bed early.

- **Encourage regular daily naps.** Daily naps are important. An energetic child can find it difficult to go through the day without a rest break. A napless child will often wake up cheerful but become progressively fussier or hyperalert as the day goes on.
- **Set your child's biological clock.** Take advantage of your child's biology so that she's actually tired when bedtime arrives. Expose your child to bright morning light to push the biological "go" button—the one that says, "Time to wake up and be active." Then align your child's sleepiness with bedtime by dimming the lights during the hour before bedtime.
- **Develop a consistent bedtime routine.** Routines create security and prevent battles. A consistent, peaceful bedtime routine allows your child to transition from the motion of the day to the tranquil state of sleep. An organized routine helps you coordinate the specifics in a peaceful manner.
- **Create a cozy sleep environment.** Where your child sleeps can be a key to quality sleep. Make certain the mattress is comfortable, the blankets are warm, the room temperature is right, pajamas are comfy, and the bedroom is welcoming.
- **Provide the right nutrition.** Foods can affect energy level and sleepiness. The right food choices can bring better sleep. Sugar, junk food, and soda pop in the few hours before bedtime can affect sleep. Provide a healthy prebedtime snack, such as whole wheat toast and cheese, a bagel and peanut butter, an apple and cheese, oatmeal with bananas, or yogurt with low-sugar granola.
- **Help your child to be healthy and fit.** Too much TV watching and a lack of activity prevents good sleep. Children who get ample daily exercise fall asleep more quickly, sleep better, stay asleep longer, and wake up feeling refreshed. But avoid activity in the hour before bedtime, since exercise can be stimulating.
- **Help your child relax.** A child who is listening to a parent read a book or tell a story, or one who is listening to peaceful

music, will tend to lie still and listen. This quiet stillness allows her to become sleepy.

What Not to Do

• **Don't keep doing what you're doing if it isn't working.** In order for your child's sleep issues to be resolved, you'll need to make changes in your current routine. Examine what's *not* working, and then make a brand-new plan.

• **Don't discipline your child for not sleeping well.** Sleep issues are resolved more effectively and peacefully when you take a positive, proactive approach to them.

• **Don't ignore the problem or think it will resolve itself.** If sleep issues are upsetting your household, take a look at the solutions in my books on this topic: *The No-Cry Sleep Solution: Gentle Ways to Help Your Baby Sleep Through the Night* and *The No-Cry Sleep Solution for Toddlers and Preschoolers: Gentle Ways to Stop Bedtime Battles and Improve Your Child's Sleep.*

Sleep Issues—Naps

See also: Sleep Issues—Bedtime

> My daughter refuses to nap, but I suspect that she still needs one. How can I convince her to sleep?

Think About It

Naps are important for your child's health and growth. A nap refreshes a child so that she can maintain her energy for the rest of the day. Studies show that children who nap are more adaptable, have longer attention spans, and are less fussy than those who don't nap.

What to Do

- **Determine if your child needs a nap.** There are some signs that tell you that your child would benefit from a nap. If she wakes up happy but gets cranky later, if she has more temper tantrums from after dinner until bedtime, and if she routinely falls asleep in the car or when watching TV, she's telling you that a daily nap is a great idea.

- **Figure out how much nap time your child needs.** Children differ in the amount of sleep they require—but most have similar needs. Toddlers usually need one to three hours of nap time, and preschoolers can use one to two hours. Many kindergarteners benefit from an hour or so of nap time. Your child's behavior is a good indicator. When in doubt try for a nap, since even if your child does not sleep the quiet time can help a child feel refreshed.

• **Change the timing and length of naps.** Timing of naps is important. A late nap or an excessively long nap will prevent your child from being tired at bedtime. Alternatively, a nap that's too short won't meet your child's sleep needs.

• **Prepare for a better nap.** Provide a healthy lunch or snack before the nap. Have a quiet, prenap routine, such as reading a book or having a massage. Keep the room dark. Play lullabies or white noise during the nap. Dress your child in comfortable clothes. Be sure that physical discomfort (teething, allergies, etc.) isn't preventing sleep.

• **Watch for signs of tiredness.** Tired children fall asleep easily. But if you miss these signals children become *overtired* and then are unable to sleep. Your child may show signs such as losing interest in playtime, becoming whiny or fussy, losing patience, having tantrums, rubbing eyes, yawning, caressing a "lovey" or blanket, or asking to nurse or for a pacifier or bottle.

• **Establish a nap routine.** Once you've created a schedule that works with your child's periods of tiredness, follow a simple but

Mother-Speak

"I really believe that the quiet hour is important to my children's sense of equilibrium in the day. Even when my son Eliot doesn't sleep, it gives him practice at being awake and quiet in his bedroom, which helps him lie quietly in the evening before he drops off to sleep. Equally important, it gives me a break as well. That one hour in the day is my sanctuary. I'm going to defend it for as long as I can!"

—Julie, mother to Eliot, age 3, and Oliver, age 2

specific nap routine. Your child will be comfortable with a pattern to her day. She may even predict when nap time approaches and willingly cooperate with you.

• **Recognize when nap routines change.** Children's sleep needs change over time. The routine that you set up today won't be the same one you're using a year from now. Be adaptable!

What Not to Do

• **Don't assume your child doesn't need a nap.** Most children up to age four or five benefit from a daily nap, even if they resist the idea.

• **Don't skip naps in hope of having an earlier or easier bedtime.** The idea of keeping a child up all day to make him extra tired for bedtime almost always backfires. Good nap-time sleep can actually improve night sleep.

• **Don't keep a nap schedule that isn't working.** Over time, children change from taking two naps to one and eventually to none. In between those time periods the schedule may change day to day. In addition, the activity of the day might warrant a longer, shorter, earlier, or later nap. Your child's daily behavior is the best indicator of whether he needs a nap.

Swearing, Bad Language, and Bathroom Jokes

See also: Backtalk; Manners

> My son thinks it's hysterical to talk about (and mimic!) bodily functions and waste products in a grossly funny way. He also finds it very funny to use swear words.

Think About It

Children find jokes about private body parts, waste products, and body sounds hysterically funny. They also figure out at a very young age that certain words have a distinctively forbidden aura. Many children go through the phase of exploring these words. While normal, it is socially inappropriate, and the sooner you take action the sooner it will stop.

What to Do

• **Ignore the first offense.** If your child innocently injects the word into his conversation, he may just be repeating something he heard. Ignoring it may be the best first defense. If your child uses the word a second time, it's clear that he's ready to learn more about improper language.

- **Teach your child what is socially inappropriate.** Children will repeat things that they hear, even when they don't know what it means—after all, that's how they've learned all the other words in their vocabulary. Your child likely doesn't know the definition of the swear word but is using it because of mimicking someone else. Identify the word and explain, "That is not a word children use." Or, "That's not something we joke about in this house."

- **Keep an eye on siblings, friends, and other adults.** Young kids are great mynah birds. Determine where your child is picking up the swear words or off-color jokes. Friends? Older siblings? Playmates? (Certainly not from *you!*) This might be a good time to have a chat about the power and meaning of words, why people swear, and what you feel is acceptable. You can provide some appropriate alternatives to use when your son's tempted to use the wrong word.

- **Monitor TV shows and movies.** Even shows that are turned on when your child is in the room, but not intended for him, can influence his vocabulary. Children are capable of picking up background words, even when they are busy playing and don't seem to be paying attention.

What Not to Do

- **Don't laugh.** Even if it *is* funny, don't react with laughter.
- **Don't get angry.** Your child might have innocently repeated a word or phrase he heard in conversation and be confused by your anger. "Why was it okay for Daddy to say that in the car, but it's not okay for me to say it?"
- **Don't express shock or offense.** Your extremely interesting response might elicit more of the same. It's unlikely that your child understood what he was saying. This is normal childish exploration of language. It just needs to be defined and corrected.

Mother-Speak

"Abby and I had a very interesting conversation about swear words yesterday. It went like this:

Abby: Mommy, we can't say 'sh*t'?

Mommy: Well, it's not a nice word.

Abby: It hurts people's feelings?

Mommy: It can hurt people's feelings, yes.

Abby: But *you* say 'sh*t.'

Mommy (gulping): Well, ummm, yes, I have. But I only say it when I am really angry or when I'm hurt, like when I burned my thumb.

Abby (thoughtfully): Mama, if I burn *my* thumb, may I say 'sh*t'?

These days Abby is so into linguistics that she was clearly just asking for information. It's not like I could get angry with her for that!"

—Jenn, mother to Abigail, age 3

Teasing and Name Calling

See also: Playtime Behavior; Sibling Fights

My children frequently tease each other and their
friends. Sometimes they call each other names.

Think About It

Child-sized teasing is a normal way of experimenting with social
interaction and part of the process of figuring out how relationships work. It is sometimes a misguided attempt at gaining power
or covering emotional hurt. It can also be a sign of nervousness,
shyness, or confusion. Just like anything else that children must
learn, it takes time for them to understand the power of their
words and how to properly use that power.

What to Do

- **Allow children to work it through.** If the child being teased
doesn't seem bothered and there are no inappropriate or foul words
being used, then it's okay to consider this harmless childishness.
Avoid getting involved. Listen in to see if the children can work
through the problem on their own before you step in.
- **Teach.** Explain what teasing is and why it's not right. Focus
your children's attention away from the actual words used, empha-
sizing teasing in general and its inappropriateness. Discuss the fact

that a person who teases is being unkind, even if they don't mean to be unkind.

- **Redirect.** Interrupt the teasing and change the subject. Redirect the children's attention to a group activity that promotes cooperation, such as building with blocks or playing a board game.
- **Make it a family rule.** "We do not tease others." Post the rule on poster board, along with three or four other main family rules, in a central location in your home. (See Family Rules: A Key to Peace, on page 87.)
- **Teach the child who is being teased how to protect herself.** Privately discuss several options that she can use to discourage the teaser. For example, suggest that she laugh at the comment, ignore the teaser, or express her unhappiness in a confident statement. Let her know that she can come to you if she feels unable to handle it herself.

What Not to Do

- **Don't ignore adult teasing.** Make sure none of the adults in the family are teasing the children. Often adults think it's funny to tease and assume that the children think it's funny, too. Children may even laugh and act as if they enjoy the teasing, when in reality it hurts their feelings. The children in the family will model the parents' actions and tease each other in the same way they have been teased.
- **Don't assume a child who teases is being bad.** There may be underlying emotions such as embarrassment or nervousness that are causing the teasing. See if you can determine what's really happening before you jump in to correct the behavior. Once you understand the origin of the teasing, you can address that first and teach better ways to handle these emotions.

- **Don't embarrass the teaser with a public reprimand.** Interrupt the children when you hear teasing. Take the child aside for a private discussion. Firmly state your position on teasing. Request that she apologize and send her back out to play.

- **Don't forget to monitor media influences.** Keep an eye on the TV shows your child is watching. Sources of humor in some shows are sarcasm and putting people down—which are followed by big laughs. Your child may be picking up on this and adapting the technique to her own repertoire.

Toothbrushing

See also: Bath, Not Behaving In; Bath, Not Wanting One

> I have to fight to get my child to brush his teeth! It's a major disruption every morning and every night.

Think About It

Daily tooth care is vital to your child's health. Having your child brush every day is an important part of that care. And, there are ways to make the task less stressful—maybe even pleasant.

What to Do

- **Make brushing teeth a part of your routine.** Do it as part of your morning routine, such as right after your child gets dressed, and at the same time every night, such as right after putting on pajamas. If you don't miss a day, it will soon become a natural habit.
- **Model good tooth care.** Children watch their older siblings, parents, and others for cues to how they should behave. Let your child observe other people brushing their teeth, including yourself. Brush together and take advantage of your little one's desire to imitate your actions.
- **Choose the right brush.** Use a brush designed for children. While using a bigger brush may seem more efficient, it's the equivalent of sticking a hairbrush in your mouth—overwhelming.

Kyleigh, age 2

Instead, opt for the special brushes made especially for children's smaller mouths. Choose a soft-bristled brush to make brushing more pleasant and to prevent hurting your child's gums.

• **Experiment with different types of toothbrushes and toothpastes.** Search out colorful, musical toothbrushes or those with playful designs. Try an electric or battery-powered brush made especially for children. These do a great job of cleaning teeth, and your little one may enjoy the buzzing sound and tingly feeling. If you have several brushes, let your little one choose which brush to use each time he brushes.

• **Use only a small swipe of toothpaste.** Too much can be unpleasant (and unhealthy) for your child, and a tiny bit does the job.

Mother-Speak

"After many months of trying to get my son to cooperate with toothbrushing, it finally occurred to me that Elmo was on his toothbrush and I could use this to help. I mustered up the best Elmo impression I could and said, 'Elmo is REALLY hungry. Elmo heard that you ate burritos for dinner. Would you please give Elmo some, too?' Samuel smiled, giggled, and gladly opened his mouth to feed Elmo. Now he and his little sister usually run off down the hall to 'feed Elmo' before bed."

—**Morgan, mother to Samuel, age 4, and Abby, age 2**

- **Be creative.** Pretend the toothbrush is a train and the teeth a track. Make enthusiastic train noises, and encourage your child to drive the train. Give the toothbrush and teeth voices, and have them talk to each other. Make up a toothbrushing song, or use a variation of a favorite tune. There's no reason that this daily ritual can't be a fun one!

What Not to Do

- **Don't let your child off the hook to avoid the battle.** Not only can cavities develop quickly if you don't brush, but you are setting in place important lifelong habits.
- **Don't threaten future problems.** Telling a toddler he'll have to have a cavity filled at his next checkup or threatening a preschooler that he'll have dentures at age forty won't have much impact. Children can't think that far ahead.

Traveling

See also: Car Problems; Restaurant Behavior

> When we go on trips with our children, it seems to bring out their worst behavior. What should be a fun vacation turns into a trying chore.

Think About It

A new location, unusual foods, mysterious unfamiliar people, loss of household routines, and a liberal dose of excitement—all of these contribute to your children's unruly vacation behavior. There are a number of things that you can do to turn things around and have a delightful excursion with your children.

What to Do

• **Keep your normal routines.** Disruption of the familiar can create chaos with children. When planning your travel times and vacation events, try to keep four things consistent with your usual routines: morning wake-up time, nap time, mealtimes, and bedtime. Of course this isn't always possible, but the further you veer from your usual routines the more likely your children's behavior will deteriorate.

• **Have realistic expectations.** Adults are able to transform their normal behavior to vacation behavior, but children don't function this way. If your child is a picky eater at home, she'll be a picky eater on vacation. If your children argue at home, they'll argue away from home. If your child dawdles at home, she'll move slowly on vacation. When you expect something different from the norm just because you are away from home, you are setting yourself up for disappointment. Yet almost all parents fall prey to the belief that their children's behavior will magically improve because they've bought airline tickets and rented a hotel room.

- **Banish boredom.** We expect a vacation to bring all the fun our children need. However, here are many hours of unfilled time involved: waiting in lines, sitting in buses, waiting for meals to be served. Boredom is one of the main culprits for cranky children and misbehavior during trips. Prevent boredom by packing "fun bags" and keeping a few with you at all times. The party aisle of your favorite toy store has lots of inexpensive ideas to fill your bags, such as tiny plastic animals, Silly Putty, stickers, drawing paper and markers, playing cards, comic books, and miniature travel games. These toys can be used anytime you need to keep your child occupied.

- **Tell them what to expect.** In advance of your journey, let your children know what the travel plans are—how long the journey will take, the expected time of arrival, where you will sleep, and what you will do all day. The better prepared they are and the fewer the surprises, the more pleasant your children will be to travel with. For younger children, you can even role-play the trip in advance. As an example, set up chairs as an airplane in your living room. Pretend your bedroom is the hotel room. Play-act the trip, discussing what will happen when you're on vacation.

- **Have vacation rules.** Children will respond much better if they know exactly what is expected of them. At the start of the trip, or even before you leave, write down a list of rules. (Add to them as necessary as the trip goes on.) Review the rules each morning. This is a fantastic way to avoid power struggles during the day.

- **Use your parenting skills.** Remember to use all the skills you have learned. Offering choices, using 5-3-1 Go!, engaging the imagination, and having clear, specific, eye-to-eye discussions will all help prevent you from losing your patience.

What Not to Do

- **Don't expect perfection.** It doesn't matter how much money you've paid, how much time it took to plan, or how excited you are about the trip—your children's behavior will be dictated by what's inside them, not by where they are in the world. They aren't misbehaving because they are ungrateful or bad—they are just being normal children.
- **Don't be too rigid.** Relax and pick your battles. Bending a few rules is okay when you're away from home. Don't worry so much about the little things, and focus on having a good time yourself.

Yelling, Screaming, and Shouting

....

See also: Playtime Behavior

My son has one volume level:
loud!

Think About It

Many young children have an abundance of energy, and loud voices are the verbal aspect of that energy. Fortunately, most learn better volume control over time.

What to Do

- **Ask politely.** When your child gets too loud, go directly to him, get down to his eye level, and ask him to use his quiet, inside voice. Then demonstrate what you mean by saying in a quiet voice, "Talk to me in a voice like this."
- **Watch your own volume.** Children are great at modeling the communication styles they see and hear around them. Many parents don't realize how often they raise their voices at their children. Pay attention to your own voice. Do you call to him from another room? Do you raise your voice to be heard above his noise? Use your voice level to demonstrate to your child the appropriate tone he should be using.

- **Have more eye-to-eye communication.** Some children raise their voices to get your attention. To prevent this, get down to your child's level when he's talking to you and maintain eye contact as you listen.

- **Provide a time and place to yell.** Make sure your children have an outlet for their boisterous voices. Get them involved in a choir or a sports team. Take them to an indoor play arena or a large park often enough to exercise their lungs.

- **Try whispering.** Make a game of using a whispery voice to talk to each other. Practice with a quieter volume might help your child lower his.

- **Redirect your child's energy.** When your child's noise level increases and it begins to bother you, interrupt his current activity and redirect him to a quieter pursuit. Get him started on a puzzle, working with clay, making a drawing, or building with blocks.

- **Have your child's hearing checked.** A child who constantly uses a loud voice may have a problem hearing. Children who have had frequent ear infections might have a buildup of fluid that makes hearing difficult. It's always a good idea to check with a medical professional to be sure there isn't a physical problem.

- **Control your anger.** If your child's behavior upsets you, it is important to control your own anger. For tips on how to keep your cool, review Part 3, A Peaceful Home: Staying Calm and Avoiding Anger, on page 127.

What Not to Do

- **Don't raise your volume.** Your automatic response may be to yell louder than your child so that you'll be heard. Instead, use a gentle, calm voice to bring your child's level down to yours. Often, if you get your child's visual attention and begin to talk quietly, he'll stop to hear what you say. If you engage him in a quiet moment, usually the effect will last, at least for a while.

- **Don't take it personally.** Your child is *not* yelling at you, and you haven't done something wrong to encourage the yelling. Loud voices are an aspect of normal childish behavior that will likely improve over time.

- **Don't expect things to change in a day.** If yelling and screaming have become a habit, it will take some time to modify this behavior. Be patient.

Index

About the Author

Parenting educator Elizabeth Pantley is president of Better Beginnings, Inc., a family resource and education company. Elizabeth frequently speaks to parents at schools, hospitals, and parent groups around the world. Her presentations are received with enthusiasm and are praised as realistic, warm, and helpful.

She is a regular radio show guest and frequently quoted as a parenting expert in newspapers and magazines such as *Parents*, *Parenting*, *American Baby*, *Woman's Day*, *Good Housekeeping*, and *Redbook*. Elizabeth is also quoted on hundreds of parent-directed websites. She publishes a newsletter, *Parent Tips*, which is distributed in schools nationwide.

Elizabeth is the author of these popular parenting books, available in eighteen languages:

- *The No-Cry Sleep Solution: Gentle Ways to Help Your Baby Sleep Through the Night*
- *The No-Cry Sleep Solution for Toddlers and Preschoolers: Gentle Ways to Stop Bedtime Battles and Improve Your Child's Sleep*
- *The No-Cry Potty Training Solution: Gentle Ways to Help Your Child Say Good-Bye to Diapers*
- *Gentle Baby Care: No-Cry, No-Fuss, No-Worry—Essential Tips for Raising Your Baby*
- *Hidden Messages: What Our Words and Actions Are Really Telling Our Children*
- *Perfect Parenting: The Dictionary of 1,000 Parenting Tips*
- *Kid Cooperation: How to Stop Yelling, Nagging and Pleading & Get Kids to Cooperate*

Elizabeth was also a contributing author to *The Successful Child* with Dr. William and Martha Sears.

Elizabeth and her husband, Robert, live in the state of Washington, along with their four children, Angela, Vanessa, David, and Coleton, and Grama (Elizabeth's mother). Elizabeth is an involved participant in her children's school and sports activities and has served in positions as varied as softball coach and school PTA president.

For more information, excerpts, and parenting articles, visit the author's website at pantley.com/elizabeth.

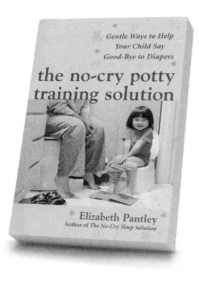